MEDITATIONS ON ST. JOHN

by
Dr. Burns K. Seeley, Ph.D.

Nihil Obstat: Rev. John A. Hardon, S.J.
Censor Deputatus
Imprimatur: Rev. Msgr. John F. Donoghue
Vicar General of the Archdiocese of Washington, D.C.
February 9, 1981

Library of Congress Card Number
81-65808

ISBN Number 0-932406-03-3

Apostolate for Family Consecration®
Catholic Familyland®
3375 County Rd. 36
Bloomingdale, OH 43910-7903
(740)-765-5500
www.familyland.org

Copyright MCMLXXXI The Apostolate for Family Consecration, Inc.

File in
The Apostolate's Prayerbook
Book A4-1, Behind Section 2, Chapter 100

or

Living Meditation and Prayerbook Series
Book A4-3, Behind Section C2, Chapter 100

Structured by Jerome F. Coniker
Edited by Dale Francis

Full color cover picture and halftone meditation pictures copyright 1955 through 1963 The Apostleship of Prayer, used by permission.

Information coding from the Coniker Communications System, copyright 1977, 1978 and 1980 Coniker Systems, Inc. used by permission.

Excerpts from The Jerusalem Bible copyright 1966 by Darton Longman & Todd, Ltd. and Doubleday and Company, Inc., used by permission of the publisher.

Copyright MCMLXXXI The Apostolate for Family Consecration, Inc.

Published by
The Apostolate for Family Consecration
The Apostolate, Box 220
Kenosha, Wisconsin 53141
Printed in U.S.A.

Table of Contents

First Week Day 1 19
First Week Day 2 26
First Week Day 3 38
First Week Day 4 49
First Week Day 5 58
First Week Day 6 73
First Week Day 7 85

Second Week Day 1 102
Second Week Day 2 111
Second Week Day 3 120
Second Week Day 4 127
Second Week Day 5 135
Second Week Day 6 147
Second Week Day 7 159

Third Week Day 1 170
Third Week Day 2 180
Third Week Day 3 188
Third Week Day 4 197
Third Week Day 5 207
Third Week Day 6 213
Third Week Day 7 224

References to Scripture 234

Prayer petitions 240

INTRODUCTION TO ST. JOHN
by
Dr. Burns K. Seeley, Ph.D.

1. Before you begin your meditative adventure into St. John's writings, take time to read these introductory pages. They will help you to cultivate the art of meditation.

2. When you meditate on Scripture, we want you to discover for yourselves Scripture's Four C's Formula for Peaceful Seed Living. It is a formula which will enable you to rise above your problems and accomplish worthy goals you never thought possible. It will also enable you to help countless suffering souls. Therefore, we are first going to spend a few minutes discussing this formula, concentrating on the nature of each of the Four C's.

3. Next, we will share with you some suggestions on how to meditate well. This will be followed by some background material on St. John, his Gospel and his three letters, which will help you to better understand the man and the message he conveys as Christ's Apostle and Evangelist.

Scripture's Four C's

4. What are Scripture's Four C's? Those of you who are already acquainted with the work of The Apostolate will no doubt know the answer, especially if you have read Volume I of our two volume work called *Scripture's Four C's Formula for Peaceful Seed Living* and our *Prayers and*

Recommended Practices book.

5. Confidence, Conscience, seed-Charity and Constancy. These are the four pillars of the peaceful seed-living formula. And we hope that the Four C's will become a permanent part of your lives so that you will always have ready access to that God-given peace which defies complete understanding.

Confidence (C-1)

6. The first C - "Confidence." When we speak of "Confidence," what do we mean? We mean a supernaturally-given trust in God, a trust in His unique plan for each of us, and a trust in the strength He will give us to accomplish this plan. Since God is completely good, He desires only what is best for us, namely, our happiness. But if we are to obtain this happiness, our trust, or confidence, must be focused on Him.

7. We also mean by confidence, a supernaturally-given ability to believe the truths which the Father has revealed for our salvation through the patriarchs, the prophets, the Apostles, and Jesus. When we use confidence to mean belief, we are using it in the same way that "faith" is used in most of the New Testament, that is, in the exclusively Christian part of the Bible.

8. Less frequently, we use confidence to mean hope, that is, hope in eternal life with God, hope in the rewards that accompany eternal life and hope in the means of obtaining eternal happiness with God.

9. It can be seen then, that we use confidence as a synonym for trust, faith and hope, which are special graces, mentioned often in the New Testament, and given by God for our salvation.

10. To sum up, The Apostolate speaks of confidence as trust in God, belief in His supernaturally revealed truths, hope in eternal life and hope in the means to obtain it.

Conscience (C-2)

11. Now, the second C - "Conscience." As used by The Apostolate for Family Consecration, conscience means a pure conscience, or one that is free from all fully deliberate sins, since these are the major obstacles to spiritual growth and a life of union or oneness with God.

12. On the other hand, while they do not prevent us from enjoying God's friendship

and a pure conscience, imperfections and half-deliberate sins are nonetheless obstacles to obtaining a purer conscience, and they can be sources of spiritual illnesses leading to mortal sins. Therefore, we should, with the aid of God's grace, seek to remove them, as well as all willful sins.

13. Throughout Scripture, we are counselled to purify our consciences by repenting of our sins so that we can grow in holiness and in God's friendship. In order to accomplish this properly, a daily in-depth self-examination for these hindrances to holiness should be undertaken.

Seed-Charity (C-3)

14. Next, our third C - "seed-Charity." Seed-charity or seed-sacrifice, or we could say seed-love, is that grace referred to in the Bible which makes it possible for us to offer ourselves fully to the true service of God and our fellow man. Put another way, we could say that seed-charity enables us to love God as He commanded us to do with all our hearts, with all our souls, with all our minds,

and with all our strength, and to love our neighbor as ourselves.

15. We of The Apostolate prefer the term "seed-charity" to simply "charity" or "love," since in modern English it is not always clear what these latter two terms mean. Thus when we prefix "seed" to charity, we wish to convey the idea of a love which is essentially sacrificial. Without this prefix, charity is often thought of solely in terms of donating time or money to some worthy cause. But activity of this sort is not always sacrificial. Also, the word "love" without the prefix "seed" could mean either romantic love, or the love of casual friendship, but neither of these has to be sacrificial either.

16. If we were to reflect on it, we would all realize that a seed is meant to sacrifice itself, or die, so that a new life, that of a plant, might emerge and eventually achieve full growth. Similarly, one who exercises sacrificial love or seed-charity dies to his selfishness, so that a new Christ-like individual can emerge and ultimately attain full growth in sanctity through a transforming union with Our Lord.

17. We do not have to look further than our own immediate environment to know where we should plant our seeds of sacrificial charity. And in doing so, we are faithfully fulfilling our responsibilities. Trials, for instance, which come upon all of us, can be sanctified by offering them to God in the spirit of seed-charity. When we plant seeds of sacrifice to meet our spiritual needs in this life, we are preparing ourselves for eternal life with God in His heavenly Kingdom. We are also achieving peaceful seed-living on earth, and we are having our material needs met as well.

Constancy (C-4)

18. Finally, the fourth C - "Constancy." By constancy we mean a special supernatural grace which allows us to persevere with a pure conscience in the Christian life, even during moments of difficult temptations. We need this grace to persevere in all acts which lead to our destiny in Heaven, but especially in the exercise of confidence and seed-charity.

19. Constancy is living in God's presence. It is a continuous vigilance over the things that please God. This includes maintaining our positive attitudes of expectations for God's love, for responses to our prayers, and for God's harvest from the charitable seeds we have planted. In a certain sense we can say that constancy is the most important of all virtues since it undergirds and reinforces all the others. Without it, all of our efforts would bear little spiritual fruit.

The Four C's

20. Now let's condense and simplify our definitions of the Four C's. Confidence is that grace which makes it possible for us to trust and hope in God, and also to believe all the supernatural truths He has revealed for our salvation.

21. By conscience, we normally mean a conscience which is pure or free of all fully deliberate sins.

22. Seed-charity is the supernatural ability to sacrifice ourselves for God by loving Him directly through prayer and worship, and also in our neighbor. We love God too by fulfilling our responsibilities and changing our trials into positive seeds of sacrifice.

23. Finally, there is constancy which is a special God-given aid that helps us persevere in the fulfillment of our Christian responsibilities and fulfill our needs so we can do God's will on earth and ultimately obtain Heaven.

Meditation

24. Making good meditations is crucial for proper spiritual development. That is why they are an integral part of The Apostolate's spiritual formation programs.

25. In general, we could say that a spiritual meditation consists simply in making a prayerful reflection on some spiritual topic or topics with the purpose of knowing and loving God better.

26. Sacred Scripture or, for that matter, any number of excellent spiritual books, can serve as focal points for meditating since they are rich sources of spiritual subject matter. We would recommend, first and foremost, however, the use of Sacred Scripture inasmuch as it is the primary source book of Christian spirituality.

27. Over the centuries, the Church has highly recommended scriptural meditation. The Second Vatican Council (1962-1965), for example, spoke of scriptural meditation as a means of dialoguing with God. Thus it noted that we speak to God when we pray and we listen to Him when we read (and meditate on) His written Word. *(Dogmatic Constitution on Divine Revelation, #25.)*

28. What are the main steps in a scriptural meditation? First, a quiet place should be found - ideally in a church in the presence of the Blessed Sacrament. But, for many, this may not be practical on a regular basis. Consequently, you might choose an isolated room in your own home, such as a bedroom.

29. You should precede your meditation with a prayer to God the Holy Spirit for help to make your meditation fruitful. And if you have not already done so, it would be well to examine your conscience and confess your sins so that there will be no obstacles to the action of God's grace within you. One more thing - it is best to meditate at the same time each day. This makes it easier for meditation to become a habit and therefore a normal part of your life.

30. Now, placing the Scripture reading you are going to meditate on in front of you, you should be ready to begin. It is best to read slowly and deliberately, and if you feel moved to do so, to pause from time to time, to reflect on the sentences or passage just read.

31. What do they mean? What is God saying to you and to your families through them? What acts of charity do they suggest? Perhaps they suggest more fervent prayers, or greater generosity to those closest to you, or some special act of seed-charity for someone you have wrongfully injured.

32. Also when meditating try to find within the Scripture readings, words and ideas which suggest the Four C's. You will probably be surprised to see how often they occur. Confidence, as we have already mentioned, can be seen in words such as "faith," "hope" and "trust." Conscience, or a pure conscience, is suggested immediately by terms such as "pure heart," and "honest and good heart." And it is suggested indirectly by many references to sins which must be repented of before a pure conscience can be secured. The idea of seed-charity is found especially in the frequent use of "love" - and the concept of constancy can be found in the use of words such as "persevere" and "endure."

33. Note also in the margin of your Scripture readings, the numbered C's. C-1 represents confidence. C-2 stands for conscience. C-3 stands for seed-charity, and C-4 represents constancy. These are guides for you in discovering the Four C's in the adjacent Scripture passages. You will undoubtedly discover other references to them as well.

34. It is important that your meditations be forms of prayer, and the subject matter of each prayer should be whatever the Holy Spirit suggests to you while meditating. Perhaps you will be led to express sorrow for your sins, or gratitude for having a loving God, One Who was willing to become man to suffer and die for us. Or reflecting on Scripture may bring to mind those who could

use our prayers and other sacrificial acts. Also be sure to note the suggestions for meditating contained in the video presentations of the Neighborhood Peace of Heart Forums.

35. During the three weeks of the present spiritual leadership program, when you have completed your daily meditation and your prayers, read also the prepared companion meditation found in this book, in the same slow, deliberate manner. Both this and your own meditation will be based on the same Scripture passages.

36. The purpose of using the companion meditations is to give you additional insights into the meaning of God's words and His will for you, your family and others. You may find, too, that they will suggest further sacrificial acts to perform for God and for others. Don't forget that true penance is first of all the faithful fulfillment of one's responsibilities in one's state in life and the offering up of one's trials as a positive seed of sacrifice for God.

37. By the way, we suggest that if you have not meditated regularly before, that, at first, you spend only fifteen to twenty minutes a day in meditation. Then we recommend that you work your way up to a half hour and then to an hour, both of which may well seem to pass rather quickly.

The Apostle St. John and His Writings: The Gospel and His Letters

38. As you may already know, for the next three weeks we are asking you to meditate on the Gospel according to St. John and on his three letters. In a moment we will share with you some of the distinctive characteristics of these writings. Right now, however, let's look at a brief sketch of the author himself.

39. St. John the Apostle, also known as St. John the Evangelist and the Beloved Disciple, was the son of Zebedee, a Galilean fisherman. John and his brother, James, also became fishermen, but later they became disciples of St. John the Baptist. When Jesus began His public ministry, however, He called them to leave the Baptist and to follow Him.

40. Among the members of the Twelve Apostles, St. John was one of those closest to Our Lord, and together with St. Peter, St. John played an especially prominent role in founding and guiding the Church after Pentecost.

41. During the formative period of the early Church, St. John and the other Apostles spent about twelve years working in Palestine. At the end of this period, a

persecution initiated by King Herod Agrippa led the Apostles to evangelize other areas of the Roman Empire.

42. St. John returned to Jerusalem, about A.D. 51, to attend the Apostolic Council which dealt with the problem of admitting Gentiles into the Church. Eventually, according to early tradition, St. John went to Asia Minor where he governed the Churches of that area from Ephesus. While residing there, he is said to have written the Gospel that bears his name.

43. At some point during the reign of Emperor Domitian (A.D. 51-96), early Church writers tell us that St. John was banished to the Greek island of Patmos in the Aegaen Sea. It was here that he wrote the Book of Revelation, also known as the Apocalypse.

44. After the death of Domitian, St. John reportedly returned to Ephesus where he died about four years later.

45. John is held to have been the youngest of the Apostles. He was also a model of virginity and a strong adversary of heretical, or false, Christian doctrine. And according to tradition, among the Apostles, John alone died a natural death, and this at an advanced age.

The Gospel

46. The Gospel according to St. John is a divinely inspired account of the life and teaching of Jesus Christ written from the viewpoint of the Beloved Disciple. As is true of the Gospel accounts of the other Evangelists, St. John's version proclaims the Good News that Jesus, the Messiah, is God the Son Who became man for our salvation. John's Gospel, however, contains certain terms not found in the Gospels of Matthew, Mark and Luke.

47. We have in mind, for example, contrasting words such as "truth" and "lie," "light" and "darkness," "angel of light" and "angel of darkness." And only St. John repeatedly stresses the need for mutual love and unity among Christ's followers.

48. Moreover, St. John alone describes Jesus as the Word of God. It is this Word Who was sent to earth by the express desire of the Father in order to give mankind eternal life with God. This is the theme that dominates all of St. John's Gospel and reveals the Father's love for mankind.

49. St. John gives prominence as well to God the Holy Spirit, the Spirit of Truth through Whom the risen and glorified Christ would govern His Church.

50. Two more distinctive themes in St. John's Gospel are the devil and the world, that is, the world alienated from God and governed by satan.

51. St. John also emphasizes certain features more than do the other Gospel writers. For instance, he took more pains to note the significance of key events in Jesus' life and the significance of all He said and did. Moreover, John alone spoke of Jesus' miracles as "signs," pointing to Him as the Messiah and as the Son of God.

52. We note, too, in St. John's Gospel a greater interest in the sacraments and in worship. Thus we find Our Lord's discussion with Nicodemus on Baptism, and His discourse on the Eucharist. And we find the theme of Christ's sacrificial suffering and death replacing the Jewish Passover Feast.

The Letters

53. The three letters in the New Testament that bear John's name are quite similar to his Gospel in terms of their style and concern for correct doctrine.

54. The First Letter, containing five chapters, is the longest and most important. It was written for Churches being threatened with false teaching. Specifically, John writes that God is Light and it is in this Light that we

must walk if we want fellowship with Him. God is also holy. Thus we must be holy as well if we are to be His children. John states, too, that God is Love, and if we are to share in His love, we must love one another.

55. Concerning Christ, St. John writes that He is the Father's Word Who revealed Himself to men. Christ is also the Son of God, God's only-begotten Son, Who was sent into the world to manifest God's love for us.

56. St. John notes too that Jesus sacrificed His life for us by the shedding of His Blood. Thus He is our Advocate with the Father for the forgiveness of our sins. Moreover, we learn that Jesus is Life, Eternal Life.

57. We discover as well in the First Letter that a Christian is given new life, a life which shares an eternal relationship with God. Furthermore, John says Christians are the children of God in Whom God lives, who after life in this world will see Him as He is.

58. This new relationship with God, however, is conditional. It can be severed by sin. Therefore, sins must be avoided and God's commandments are to be kept, especially the commandments to love God and to love one another unselfishly. St. John notes, specifically, too, that we can forfeit our union with God by denying that Christ is the Son of God and by conforming to the spirit of the world.

59. St. John's Second Letter is addressed to "the lady, the chosen one, and to her children." Some scholars believe that it is, in fact, addressed to a local Church under John's jurisdiction, rather than to a private family as such. They reason that this is suggested by the context of the letter, and especially by the final verse which is said to refer to a sister Church: "Greetings to you from the children of your sister, the chosen one." *(2 John 13)*

60. This very brief epistle exhorts the recipients to practice seed-charity and to avoid false teachers.

61. The Third Letter of St. John is also quite short. Addressed to an unknown, Gaius, it praises him for his character and activity. His charity towards recently encountered missionaries is especially commended. St. John also lauds a man named Demetrius for his Christ-like behavior. A certain Diotrophes, however, is faulted for refusing to welcome and assist the aforementioned missionaries.

62. St. John's Second and Third letters both close with a wish to meet personally with the intended readers.

Peaceful Seed Living Prayer and Meditation Book, Volume I

63. At the end of each of the following companion meditations, which immediately follow this Introduction, note the references to Volume I of the *Peaceful Seed Living* prayer and meditation book. Be sure to read them. These will give you further insights into the spirituality of The Apostolate for Family Consecration, including the spirituality of consecration and that of Scripture's 4 C's. You will also receive information about the structure of The Apostolate.

WEEK 1 DAY 1
The Gospel of St. John
Chapter 1:1-18

THE GOSPEL ACCORDING TO Saint John

PROLOGUE

1 **1** In the beginning was the Word:
the Word was with God
and the Word was God.
2 He was with God in the beginning.
3 Through him all things came to be,
not one thing had its being but through him.
4 All that came to be had life in him
and that life was the light of men,
5 a light that shines in the dark,
a light that darkness could not overpower.*a* (C2)

6 A man came, sent by God.
His name was John.
7 He came as a witness, (C3)
as a witness to speak for the light,
so that everyone might believe through (C1)
him.
8 He was not the light,
only a witness to speak for the light. (C3)

9 The Word was the true light
that enlightens all men;
and he was coming into the world.
10 He was in the world
that had its being through him,
and the world did not know him.
11 He came to his own domain
and his own people did not accept him. (C2)

19

12 But to all who did accept him
he gave power to become children of God,
to all who believe in the name of him (C1)
13 who was born not out of human stock
or urge of the flesh
or will of man
but of God himself.
14 The Word was made flesh,
he lived among us,*b*
and we saw his glory,

the glory that is his as the only Son of the Father,
full of grace and truth.

15 John appears as his witness. He proclaims: (C3)
"This is the one of whom I said:
He who comes after me
ranks before me
because he existed before me."

16 Indeed, from his fullness we have, all of us, received—
yes, grace in return for grace,
17 since, though the Law was given through Moses,
grace and truth have come through Jesus Christ.
18 No one has ever seen God;
it is the only Son, who is nearest to the Father's heart,
who has made him known.

Week 1 Day 1
Four C's Meditations
on St. John 1:1-18

1. Jesus, we want to thank You for inspiring Your Beloved Disciple, St. John, to put into writing accounts of Your life and teaching. We are especially thankful for those passages not found elsewhere in the New Testament, since they give us a more complete picture of You and Your doctrine. We are also grateful, Lord, for St. John's unmistakable teaching that You are the eternal Son of God Who became man so that we might share in Your divine life forever.

2. Lord, among the New Testament writers, John alone refers to You as the Word of God, that is, the Word of the Father.*(1)* At first sight this title appears to be a bit strange, since it seems more appropriate for an impersonal object than for You, a personal Being. However, when we realize that St. John was writing for non-Jews familiar with Greek philosophy, the use of this name makes more sense.

3. What we mean is that some Greek philosophers held that a God-like being, or "Word," coming from the eternal God was responsible for the formation and maintenance of the universe. St. John, on the other hand, wrote to let his readers know that God had revealed that the Word of God, spoken of by the philosophers, was not only God-like, but He was God Himself, the Son of

God. And it was this personal and loving Being Who actually created the universe and keeps it in existence.

4. Moreover, Jesus, St. John said that while remaining as the eternal Word of God You also became a human being. You did this in order to sacrifice Yourself for us on the altar of the Cross and prepare us for eternal life in Your heavenly Kingdom. Thank You, Jesus, for being the Word of God by Whom the Father "In the beginning...created the heavens and earth."*(2) (See Father Hardon's "The Catholic Catechism," pp. 70-77, for further information on the creation and maintenance of the universe.)*

5. Jesus, we cannot help but be awestruck by the fact that not only did You create the entire universe and everything in it, but that You continually keep it in existence through the power of Your love. Not only that, You never fail to love us humans even when we reject You over and over again through our sins. You love mankind so much that You even humbled Yourself to become one of us in order to lead us to Your Kingdom. Lord, help us to realize how much You love us.

Especially, help us to remember often Your suffering and death on the Cross for our salvation. And may we never forget the many blessings You shower on us every day through the merits of Your Most Precious Blood. We thank You, too, for the symbol of Your Sacred Heart which is a constant reminder of Your sacrificial love on our behalf.

6. Jesus, Word of God, Word of the Father, pray for us sinners who so quickly reject Your love and turn toward our own selfish desires. Constantly remind us of Your selfless love symbolized by the image of Your Sacred Heart, and bring to our minds, from time to time, the horrors of hell where eternal pain and sorrow await those who do not strive to imitate Your earthly life, a life characterized by seed-charity. Help us to realize that we will live forever in either Heaven or hell and that the choice is ours.

7. Most Sacred Heart of Jesus, St. John also described You as the Light that lightens all men.(3) Thus when we meditate on Your

life of sacrificial love, and on Your teaching, we are shown the way out of the darkness of sin into the eternal light of Heaven.

8. Jesus, in our reading for today, we noted the prominence given to Your cousin, St. John the Baptist. He was said to be one who bore witness to You so that others might accept You as Savior and Lord.*(4)* In fact, because of his testimony two of his own followers became Your disciples, one of them being St. Andrew. This reminds us of Your teaching in St. Matthew's Gospel where You tell us that we too are called to bear witness to You as Savior and Lord so that others might come to know and love You.

9. "So if anyone declares himself for me in the presence of men, I will declare myself for him in the presence of my Father in heaven. But the one who disowns me in the presence of men, I will disown in the presence of my Father in Heaven."*(5)*

10. Lord, help us to bear witness to You as opportunities arise. May we never be ashamed or too afraid to do so. Certainly, there will probably be those who will laugh at us. Some might even threaten us. But if we persist in bearing witness to You among family members, friends, acquaintances, and neighbors, some will undoubtedly be brought to You and to salvation. Surely, their salvation is worth some risk on our part. Also, Lord, continually remind us that if we refuse to bear witness to You, we risk losing our own salvation which You earned for us on the Cross.*(6)*

11. Most Sacred Heart of Jesus, we adore You. Help us to love You more and more. Amen.

Try to read these Scripture passages and meditations several times a day in a reflective manner. Each time you do so, the Holy Spirit will give you more insights.

Please read the introduction to Mother Teresa immediately following the table of contents of Peaceful Seed Living, Volume I.

WEEK 1 DAY 2
The Gospel of St. John
Chapters 1:19-3:21

I. THE FIRST PASSOVER

A. THE OPENING WEEK

The witness of John

19 This is how John appeared as a witness. When the Jews[c] sent priests and Levites from
20 Jerusalem to ask him, "Who are you?" ·he not only declared, but he declared quite
21 openly, "I am not the Christ." ·"Well then," they asked, "are you Elijah?"[d] "I am not," (c3) he said. "Are you the Prophet?"[e] He an-
22 swered, "No." ·So they said to him, "Who are you? We must take back an answer to those who sent us. What have you to say
23 about yourself?" ·So John said, "I am, as Isaiah prophesied:

a voice that cries in the wilderness:
Make a straight way for the Lord."[f]

24 Now these men had been sent by the Phari-
25 sees, ·and they put this further question to him, "Why are you baptizing if you are not the Christ, and not Elijah, and not the
26 prophet?" ·John replied, "I baptize with water; but there stands among you—unknown
27 to you—·the one who is coming after me; and (c2)
28 I am not fit to undo his sandal-strap." ·This happened at Bethany, on the far side of the Jordan, where John was baptizing.
29 The next day, seeing Jesus coming toward him, John said, "Look, there is the lamb of (c1) God that takes away the sin of the world.

---

c. In Jn this usually indicates the Jewish religious authorities who were hostile to Jesus; but occasionally the Jews as a whole. **d.** Whose return was expected, Ml 3:23-24. **e.** The Prophet greater than Moses who was expected as Messiah, on an interpretation of Dt 18:15. **f.** Is 40:3

JOHN

30 This is the one I spoke of when I said: A man is coming after me who ranks before me be-
31 cause he existed before me. •I did not know him myself, and yet it was to reveal him to Israel that I came baptizing with water."
32 John also declared, "I saw the Spirit coming down on him from heaven like a dove and
33 resting on him. •I did not know him myself, but he who sent me to baptize with water had said to me, 'The man on whom you see the Spirit come down and rest is the one who is
34 going to baptize with the Holy Spirit.' •Yes, I have seen and I am the witness that he is (c3) the Chosen One of God."

The first disciples

35 On the following day as John stood there
36 again with two of his disciples, •Jesus passed, and John stared hard at him and said, "Look,
37 there is the lamb of God." •Hearing this, the (c1)
38 two disciples followed Jesus. •Jesus turned round, saw them following and said, "What (c3) do you want?"* They answered, "Rabbi"— which means Teacher—"where do you
39 live?" •"Come and see," he replied; so they went and saw where he lived, and stayed with him the rest of that day. It was about the tenth hour.*g*

40 One of these two who became followers of Jesus after hearing what John had said was
41 Andrew, the brother of Simon Peter. •Early next morning, Andrew met his brother and said to him, "We have found the Messiah"—
42 which means the Christ—•and he took Simon to Jesus. Jesus looked hard at him and said, "You are Simon son of John; you are to be called Cephas"—meaning Rock.

43 The next day, after Jesus had decided to leave for Galilee, he met Philip and said,
44 "Follow me." •Philip came from the same town, Bethsaida, as Andrew and Peter.
45 Philip found Nathanael*h* and said to him, "We have found the one Moses wrote about (c1) in the Law, the one about whom the prophets

wrote: he is Jesus son of Joseph, from
46 Nazareth." •"From Nazareth?" said Nathanael. "Can anything good come from that place?" "Come and see," replied Philip.
47 When Jesus saw Nathanael coming he said of him, "There is an Israelite who deserves
48 the name, incapable of deceit." •"How do you know me?" said Nathanael. "Before Philip came to call you," said Jesus, "I saw
49 you under the fig tree." •Nathanael answered, "Rabbi, you are the Son of God, you are the
50 King of Israel." •Jesus replied, "You believe (C1) that just because I said: I saw you under the fig tree. You will see greater things than
51 that." •And then he added, "I tell you most solemnly, you will see heaven laid open and, above the Son of Man, the angels of God ascending and descending."

The wedding at Cana

1 2 Three days later there was a wedding at Cana in Galilee. The mother of Jesus was
2 there, •and Jesus and his disciples had also
3 been invited. •When they ran out of wine, since the wine provided for the wedding was all finished, the mother of Jesus said to him,
4 "They have no wine." •Jesus said, "Woman, why turn to me? My hour has not come yet."
5 His mother said to the servants, *"Do what-*

6 ever he tells you."ᵃ ·There were six stone water jars standing there, meant for the ablutions that are customary among the Jews: each could hold twenty or thirty gallons.
7 Jesus said to the servants, "Fill the jars with water," and they filled them to the brim.
8 "Draw some out now," he told them, "and
9 take it to the steward." ·They did this; the steward tasted the water, and it had turned into wine. Having no idea where it came from—only the servants who had drawn the water knew—the steward called the bridegroom
10 ·and said, "People generally serve the best wine first, and keep the cheaper sort till the guests have had plenty to drink; but you have kept the best wine till now."
11 This was the first of the signs given by Jesus: it was given at Cana in Galilee. He let his glory be seen, and his disciples believed
12 in him. ·After this he went down to Capernaum with his mother and the brothers, but they stayed there only a few days.

B. THE PASSOVER

The cleansing of the Temple

13 Just before the Jewish Passover Jesus went
14 up to Jerusalem, ·and in the Temple he found people selling cattle and sheep and pigeons, and the money changers sitting at their counters
15 there. ·Making a whip out of some cord, he drove them all out of the Temple, cattle and sheep as well, scattered the money changers' coins, knocked their tables over
16 and said to the pigeon-sellers, "Take all this out of here and stop turning my Father's
17 house into a market." ·Then his disciples remembered the words of scripture: *Zeal for
18 your house will devour me.*ᵇ ·The Jews intervened and said, "What sign can you show us
19 to justify what you have done?" ·Jesus answered, "Destroy this sanctuary, and in three
20 days I will raise it up." ·The Jews replied, "It has taken forty-six years to build this sanctu-

JOHN

ary:*c* are you going to raise it up in three
21 days?" ·But he was speaking of the sanctuary
22 that was his body, ·and when Jesus rose from
the dead, his disciples remembered that he (C1)
had said this, and they believed the scripture
and the words he had said.

23 During his stay in Jerusalem for the Passover many believed in his name when they
24 saw the signs that he gave, ·but Jesus knew
them all and did not trust himself to them;
25 he never needed evidence about any man; he
could tell what a man had in him.

C. THE MYSTERY OF THE SPIRIT REVEALED TO A MASTER IN ISRAEL

The conversation with Nicodemus

1 There was one of the Pharisees called
2 Nicodemus, a leading Jew, ·who came to
Jesus by night and said, "Rabbi, we know that
you are a teacher who comes from God; for (C1)
no one could perform the signs that you do
3 unless God were with him." ·Jesus answered:

JOHN

"I tell you most solemnly,
unless a man is born from above,
he cannot see the kingdom of God."

4 Nicodemus said, "How can a grown man be born? Can he go back into his mother's
5 womb and be born again?" ·Jesus replied:

"I tell you most solemnly,
unless a man is born through water and the Spirit,
he cannot enter the kingdom of God:
6 what is born of the flesh is flesh;
what is born of the Spirit is spirit.
7 Do not be surprised when I say:
You must be born from above.
8 The wind blows wherever it pleases;
you hear its sound,
but you cannot tell where it comes from or where it is going.
That is how it is with all who are born of the Spirit."

9 "How can that be possible?" asked
10 Nicodemus. ·"You, a teacher in Israel, and you do not know these things!" replied Jesus.

11 "I tell you most solemnly,
we speak only about what we know (C2)
and witness only to what we have seen
and yet you people reject our evidence. (C2)
12 If you do not believe me
when I speak about things in this world, (C2)
how are you going to believe me
when I speak to you about heavenly things? (C1)
13 No one has gone up to heaven
except the one who came down from heaven,
the Son of Man who is in heaven;
and the Son of Man must be lifted up
14 as Moses lifted up the serpent in the desert,
15 so that everyone who believes may have eternal life in him. (C1)
16 Yes, God loved the world so much
that he gave his only Son,

so that everyone who believes in him may not (C1)
   be lost
but may have eternal life.
17 For God sent his Son into the world
not to condemn the world,
but so that through him the world might be
   saved.
18 No one who believes in him will be con- (C1)
   demned;
but whoever refuses to believe is condemned
   already,
because he has refused to believe (C2)
in the name of God's only Son.
19 On these grounds is sentence pronounced:
that though the light has come into the world
men have shown they prefer
   darkness to the light
because their deeds were evil. (C2) (C2)
20 And indeed, everybody who does wrong
hates the light and avoids it, (C2)
for fear his actions should be exposed;
21 but the man who lives by the truth (C3)
comes out into the light,
so that it may be plainly seen that what he
   does is done in God."

Week 1 Day 2
Four C's Meditations
on John 1:19-3:21

1. Again today, Lord, we encountered in our Scripture reading the witnessing of St. John the Baptist. We were inspired by his strong faith in You as the Messiah. It was this faith, for instance, which led him to humbly state that he was not worthy even to undo the straps on Your sandals. But more importantly, his faith led him to point to You and exclaim that You were the Lamb of God Who takes away the sins of the world.*(7)*

2. Yes, Jesus, You are the sacrificial Lamb Who offered Yourself to the Father on the Cross so that we might have our sins forgiven and gain access to divine friendship. As St. Peter declared, "Why, Christ himself, innocent though he was, had died once for sins, died for the guilty, to lead us to God."*(8)* And St. Paul wrote:

3. "We were still helpless when at his appointed moment Christ died for sinful men. It is not easy to die even for a good man - though of course for someone really worthy, a man might be prepared to die - but what proves that God loves us is that Christ died for us while we were still sinners."*(9)*

4. Finally, Lord, we recall Your words recorded by St. John: "A man can have no greater love than to lay down his life for his friends."*(10)*

5. Most Sacred Heart of Jesus, You are the perfect example of seed-charity. You sacrificed Your life on the Cross with no other motive than that we might have eternal happiness. Yet when we examine our own motives for helping others, we find that they are often less than completely selfless. We note motives tinged with desires to put others in our debt, to gain their favor and to promote our own ambitions. Lord, may we become much more like you. May we learn to be innocent "lambs" willing to sacrifice ourselves for others, solely for their own benefit. Help us to see and love You in all those You bring into our lives. May this especially be the case with the members of our families and with those who hurt us.

6. Jesus, in chapter two, we read of Your turning water into wine at the wedding feast at Cana. St. John called this, Your first miracle, a sign.*(11)* And indeed, it was, because it pointed to You as the Messiah and enabled Your disciples to believe in You. Elsewhere in our Scripture reading for today, St. John referred to all of Your miracles as

signs. "...many believed in his name when they saw the signs that he gave."*(12)* And we learn from St. Mark that after Your Ascension into Heaven, the Apostles "preached everywhere, the Lord working with them and confirming the word (of the Gospel) by the signs that accompanied it."*(13)*

7. Lord, may those who have witnessed miracles performed in Your Name remember them when faced with severe temptations and hardships. In this way, their faith will be strengthened and renewed.

8. Next, Jesus, we read St. John's account of the cleansing of the Jerusalem Temple.*(14)* You rightfully drove the vendors and money changers from Your Father's house, since they were desecrating it with their greed. This incident brings to mind St. Paul's teaching that our bodies are temples of the Holy Spirit which illicit sexual acts defile.*(15)* And You, Lord, expressed a similar idea when You said:

9. "But the things that come out of the mouth come from the heart and it is these

that make a man unclean. For from the heart come evil intentions: murder, adultery, fornication, theft, perjury, slander. These are the things that make a man unclean."*(16)*

10. Lord, help us to remain pure and holy in Your sight. But if we should defile ourselves with our sins, please inspire us to immediately repent so that we can receive Your forgiveness and be Your consecrated instruments in this life and the next.*(17)*

11. Jesus, in chapter three of St. John's Gospel You spoke of the necessity of Baptism for entering the Kingdom of Heaven. You also stressed the importance of accepting on faith Your doctrines which neither our senses nor reason alone can verify.*(18)* *(See "The Catholic Catechism," p. 209, for information about Jesus' teaching on the Kingdom of Heaven.)*

12. Basically, You expect us to believe You since You are worthy of belief. Your sinless life on earth and Your miracles, particularly the miracle of Your bodily Resurrection from the dead, all point to the fact that we can rely on Your testimony. Moreover, the lives of Your saints, and the miracles they performed in Your Name, also attest to Your credibility.

13. Jesus, always give us, through Your Church, the supernatural gift of faith so we can believe in You and Your doctrine without self-evident proof.

14. Lord, those who have studied and meditated on Your life and teaching with

sincerity and an open mind, and have experienced You working in their lives, cannot reasonably reject Your claim to be the divine Savior. However, there may be times when some will be tempted to deny You because of their attachment to certain sins. And some may be tempted to give up their faith in You when they find themselves undergoing great trials and difficulties. Nonetheless, the Church and Scripture assure us how much You love and care for all men, and that you will be with them in all their trials and difficulties even to the end of time.(19) As a matter of fact, trials and difficulties in life are opportunities for confirming Your existence, since by seeking Your help those who suffer will be able to detect Your presence in their lives as You supply aid and bring them nearer to You.

15. Please, Jesus, may all of our sufferings serve to draw us closer to Your Sacred Heart and make us more like Yourself, Who willingly suffered for the salvation of souls. *(For an analysis of Christian suffering see "The Catholic Catechism," pp. 431-432.)*

Try to read these Scripture passages and meditations several times a day in a reflective manner. Each time you do so, the Holy Spirit will give you more insights.

Please read the foreword by Dale Francis in our Peaceful Seed Living book, Volume I.

**WEEK 1 DAY 3
The Gospel of St. John
Chapters 3:22-4:54**

II. JOURNEYS IN SAMARIA AND GALILEE

John bears witness for the last time

22 After this, Jesus went with his disciples into the Judaean countryside and stayed with
23 them there and baptized. ·At the same time (C3) John was baptizing at Aenon*a* near Salim, where there was plenty of water, and people
24 were going there to be baptized. ·This was before John had been put in prison.
25 Now some of John's disciples had opened a discussion with a Jew about purification,
26 so they went to John and said, "Rabbi, the man who was with you on the far side of the Jordan, the man to whom you bore witness, is baptizing now; and everyone is going to
27 him." ·John replied:

"A man can lay claim
only to what is given him from heaven.

38

JOHN

28 "You yourselves can bear me out: I said: I myself am not the Christ; I am the one who has been sent in front of him.

29 "The bride is only for the bridegroom;
and yet the bridegroom's friend,
who stands there and listens,
is glad when he hears the bridegroom's voice.
This same joy I feel, and now it is complete. (C3)
30 He must grow greater,
I must grow smaller. (C3)
31 He who comes from above
is above all others;
he who is born of the earth
is earthly himself and speaks in an earthly way.
He who comes from heaven
32 bears witness to the things he has seen and heard,
even if his testimony is not accepted; (C2)
33 though all who do accept his testimony (C1)
are attesting the truthfulness of God,
34 since he whom God has sent
speaks God's own words:
God gives him the Spirit without reserve.
35 The Father loves the Son
and has entrusted everything to him.
36 Anyone who believes in the Son has eternal (C1) life,
but anyone who refuses to believe in the Son will never see life:
the anger of God stays on him." (C2)

The savior of the world revealed to the Samaritans

4 1 When Jesus heard that the Pharisees had found out that he was making and baptiz-
2 ing more disciples than John—·though in fact it was his disciples who baptized, not Jesus
3 himself—·he left Judaea and went back to
4 Galilee. ·This meant that he had to cross Samaria.

5 On the way he came to the Samaritan town called Sychar,*a* near the land that Jacob gave
6 to his son Joseph. ·Jacob's well is there and Jesus, tired by the journey, sat straight down by the well. It was about the sixth hour.*b*
7 When a Samaritan woman came to draw water, Jesus said to her, "Give me a drink."
8 His disciples had gone into the town to buy
9 food. ·The Samaritan woman said to him, "What? You are a Jew and you ask me, a Samaritan, for a drink?"—Jews, in fact, do
10 not associate with Samaritans. ·Jesus replied:

"If you only knew what God is offering
and who it is that is saying to you:
Give me a drink,
you would have been the one to ask,
and he would have given you living water."

11 "You have no bucket, sir," she answered, "and the well is deep: how could you get this
12 living water? ·Are you a greater man than our father Jacob who gave us this well and drank from it himself with his sons and his cattle?"
13 Jesus replied:
"Whoever drinks this water
will get thirsty again;
14 but anyone who drinks the water that I shall give
will never be thirsty again:
the water that I shall give
will turn into a spring inside him, welling up to eternal life."

40

JOHN

15 "Sir," said the woman, "give me some of that water, so that I may never get thirsty and never have to come here again to draw wa-
16 ter." ·"Go and call your husband" said Jesus
17 to her "and come back here." ·The woman answered, "I have no husband." He said to her, "You are right to say, 'I have no hus-
18 band'; ·for although you have had five, the one you have now is not your husband. You
19 spoke the truth there." ·"I see you are a
20 prophet, sir," said the woman. ·"Our fathers (c3) worshiped on this mountain,c while you say that Jerusalem is the place where one ought
21 to worship." ·Jesus said:

"Believe me, woman, the hour is coming (c1)
when you will worship the Father
neither on this mountain nor in Jerusalem. (c3)
22 You worship what you do not know;
we worship what we do know;
for salvation comes from the Jews.
23 But the hour will come—in fact it is here already—
when true worshipers will worship the Father
in spirit and truth:
that is the kind of worshiper
the Father wants.
24 God is spirit,
and those who worship
must worship in spirit and truth."

25 The woman said to him, "I know that Messiah—that is, Christ—is coming; and when
26 he comes he will tell us everything." ·"I who am speaking to you," said Jesus, "I am he."
27 At this point his disciples returned, and were surprised to find him speaking to a woman, though none of them asked, "What do you want from her?" or, "Why are you
28 talking to her?" ·The woman put down her water jar and hurried back to the town to tell
29 the people, ·"Come and see a man who has told me everything I ever did; I wonder if

30 he is the Christ?" ·This brought people out of the town and they started walking toward him.
31 Meanwhile, the disciples were urging him,
32 "Rabbi, do have something to eat"; ·but he said, "I have food to eat that you do not know
33 about." ·So the disciples asked one another, "Has someone been bringing him food?"
34 But Jesus said:

"My food
is to do the will of the one who sent me, (C3)
and to complete his work.
35 Have you not got a saying:
Four months and then the harvest?
Well, I tell you:
Look around you, look at the fields;
already they are white, ready for harvest!
36 Already ·the reaper is being paid his wages, (C3)
already he is bringing in the grain for eternal life,
and thus sower and reaper rejoice together. (C3)
37 For here the proverb holds good:
one sows, another reaps;
38 I sent you to reap
a harvest you had not worked for. (C3)
Others worked for it; (C3)
and you have come into the rewards of their trouble."

39 Many Samaritans of that town had believed in him on the strength of the woman's

JOHN

testimony when she said, "He told me all I
40 have ever done," ·so, when the Samaritans
came up to him, they begged him to stay with
41 them. He stayed for two days, and ·when he
spoke to them many more came to believe;
42 and they said to the woman, "Now we no (C1)
longer believe because of what you told us;
we have heard him ourselves and we know
that he really is the savior of the world." (C1)

The cure of the nobleman's son

43   When the two days were over Jesus left for
44 Galilee. ·He himself had declared that there (C2)
is no respect for a prophet in his own
45 country, ·but on his arrival the Galileans received him well, having seen all that he had (C3)
done at Jerusalem during the festival which
they too had attended.

46   He went again to Cana in Galilee, where
he had changed the water into wine. Now
there was a court official there whose son was
47 ill at Capernaum ·and, hearing that Jesus had
arrived in Galilee from Judaea, he went and (C3)
asked him to come and cure his son as he was
48 at the point of death. ·Jesus said, "So you will (C2)
not believe unless you see signs and por-
49 tents!" ·"Sir," answered the official, "come
50 down before my child dies." ·"Go home," (C1)
said Jesus. "Your son will live." The man
believed what Jesus had said and started on
51 his way; ·and while he was still on the journey
back his servants met him with the news that
52 his boy was alive. ·He asked them when the
boy had begun to recover. "The fever left
him yesterday," they said, "at the seventh
53 hour." ·The father realized that this was exactly the time when Jesus had said, "Your
son will live"; and he and all his household (C1)
believed.

54   This was the second sign given by Jesus,
on his return from Judaea to Galilee.

Week 1 Day 3
Four C's Meditations
on St. John 3:22-4:54

1. Lord and Savior, during today's meditation, our attention focused on the humility of St. John the Baptist. It was this virtue, supported by his faith in You, which allowed him to see reality from the divine point of view. Thus, with reference to You, he could say, "He must grow greater, I must grow smaller. He who comes from above is above all others."(20)

2. This passage also reminds us of St. Paul's famous statement in which he too could say with true humility: "I have been crucified with Christ, and I live now not with my own life but with the life of Christ who lives in me. The life I now live in this body I live in faith: faith in the Son of God who loves me and who sacrificed himself for my sake."(21) In effect, St. Paul's on-going faith and charity allowed him to grow smaller with respect to sin, and it allowed You to grow greater within him, creating a state of continuous growth in sanctity.

3. Lord, so often our sins, especially the sin of pride, prevent us from being genuinely humble. Consequently, we become blinded to reality and fail to see our urgent need for Your love, forgiveness and grace. Please inspire us to see ourselves as You see us, so that we may see our sins and have them removed by Your saving grace. May we also see clearly the talents and virtues You have given us, and may we always use them for Your honor and glory, and for the benefit of others, as well as for the salvation of our own souls. Lord, help us, too, to grow smaller in our own eyes, so that You can increasingly enter into our lives to purify and sanctify them. Then, we will be able to say with St. Paul, "I live now not with my own life but with the life of Christ who lives in me."

4. Next, Lord, we meditated on the account of Your dialogue with the Samaritan woman at Jacob's well.(22) Unfortunately, her relationship with a man, not her husband, is all too reminiscent of similar situations in our own time. Anyone familar with the New Testament knows that You have condemned

premarital and extramarital relations. The tragedy today is that, in our supposedly Christian culture, such relationships not only exist on a wide scale, but they are often professed to be a good thing.

5. Lord, we need to stress over and over again that sex, through a gift from You, is properly expressed only within the context of a true marriage. No matter how popular premarital and extramarital sexual relationships may be, they can never receive Your approval, since they run counter to the good of societies and individuals. St. Paul described these relationships under the heading of self-indulgence. *(See "The Catholic Catechism," pp. 356-366 for information on the nature of marriage.)*

6. "When self-indulgence is at work the results are obvious: fornication, gross indecency and sexual irresponsibility; idolatry and sorcery; feuds and wrangling, jealousy, bad temper and quarrels; disagreements, factions, envy; drunkeness, orgies and similar things. I warn you now, as I warned you before: those who believe like this will not inherit the kingdom of God."*(23, 24)*

7. Lastly, Lord, while premarital and extramarital relationships can exclude one from the Kingdom of God, You will also forgive and restore to Your friendship those who sincerely repent of such acts and, in the case of Catholics, receive the sacrament of Penance. *(See "The Catholic Catechism," pp. 481 for information on this sacrament.)*

8. Help us, most merciful Jesus, to remain chaste according to our state in life. And we thank You for the powerful help in this regard which millions have received from Your Blessed Mother. *(For more on the Blessed Virgin Mary see "The Catholic Catechism," pp. 169-170.)*

9. Lord, You told the Samaritan woman that true worshippers worship the Father in spirit and in truth.*(25)* That is, true worshippers worship God in spirit with their spiritual minds, under the inspiration of the Holy Spirit. They also worship God in truth, since You, Who are the Truth, have given them the truths they need to know for their salvation. Lord, may we always worship the Father in spirit and in truth as expressions of our sincere love for Him.

10. Jesus, we noted with interest in today's reading, the incident in which You healed the official's son. When You told him that his dying son would live, he immediately believed You. Yet, in sharp contrast to this man's faith in You, how often we ourselves tend to disbelieve Your words.

11. You promised, for instance, to be with Your followers until the end of the world.*(26)* But when we are confronted with severe temptations and trials, we sometimes find it hard to believe that You are really with us, waiting for us to turn to You, so that You can come to our rescue. Or again, many find it hard to believe Your clear teaching that marriage is life-long.*(27)* This is especially true when couples experience difficulties which inevitably trouble every marriage. *(On the*

permanence of marriage, see The Catholic Catechism, Pp. 356-362.)

12. Lord, You are God. You will never let us down. You will see us safely through all of life's difficulties, provided of course, that we believe and trust in You with a pure heart. Please help us not to become discouraged. Remind us often that You are with us, always seeking to make us holy. Remind us that You are a firm Rock which we can always cling to when life's storms come our way.

13. Thank You, Jesus, for being Our Savior and Defender against the forces of evil. You will never desert us. May we never desert You.

14. Most Sacred Heart of Jesus, I believe, I adore, I trust and I love You. I ask pardon for those who do not believe, do not adore, do not trust, and do not love You. Amen.

Try to read these Scripture passages and meditations in a reflective manner every day. The Holy Spirit will reveal more insights to you each time you do so.

Please read and meditate on Chapter I, Paragraphs 1 to 22 of Peaceful Seed Living, Volume I.

**WEEK 1 DAY 4
The Gospel of St. John
Chapter 5:1-47**

III. THE SECOND FEAST AT JERUSALEM

The cure of a sick man at the Pool of Bethzatha

5 Some time after this there was a Jewish festival, and Jesus went up to Jerusalem. ²Now at the Sheep Pool in Jerusalem there is a building, called Bethzatha in Hebrew, consisting of five porticos; ³·and under these were crowds of sick people—blind, lame, paralyzed—waiting for the water to move; ⁴·for at intervals the angel of the Lord came down into the pool, and the water was disturbed, and the first person to enter the water after this disturbance was cured of any ailment he suffered from. ⁵·One man there had an illness ⁶which had lasted thirty-eight years, ·and when Jesus saw him lying there and knew he had been in this condition for a long time, he ⁷said, "Do you want to be well again?" ·"Sir," replied the sick man, "I have no one to put me into the pool when the water is disturbed; and while I am still on the way, someone else

8 gets there before me." ·Jesus said, "Get up,
9 pick up your sleeping-mat and walk." ·The man was cured at once, and he picked up his mat and walked away.

Now that day happened to be the sabbath,
10 so the Jews said to the man who had been cured, "It is the sabbath; you are not allowed
11 to carry your sleeping-mat." ·He replied, "But the man who cured me told me, 'Pick
12 up your mat and walk.' " ·They asked, "Who is the man who said to you, 'Pick up your mat
13 and walk?' " ·The man had no idea who it was, since Jesus had disappeared into the
14 crowd that filled the Temple. ·After a while Jesus met him in the Temple and said, "Now you are well again, be sure not to sin any (c2) more, or something worse may happen to
15 you." ·The man went back and told the Jews
16 that it was Jesus who had cured him. ·It was because he did things like this on the sabbath
17 that the Jews began to persecute Jesus. ·His answer to them was, "My Father goes on (c2)
18 working, and so do I." ·But that only made (c2) the Jews even more intent on killing him, because, not content with breaking the sabbath, he spoke of God as his own Father, and so made himself God's equal.
19 To this accusation Jesus replied:

"I tell you most solemnly,
the Son can do nothing by himself;
he can do only what he sees the Father doing:
and whatever the Father does the Son does too.
20 For the Father loves the Son
and shows him everything he does himself,
and he will show him even greater things than these,
works that will astonish you.
21 Thus, as the Father raises the dead and gives them life,
so the Son gives life to anyone he chooses;

JOHN

22 for the Father judges no one;
   he has entrusted all judgment to the Son, (C3)
23 so that all may honor the Son
   as they honor the Father.
   Whoever refuses honor to the Son (C2)
   refuses honor to the Father who sent him.
24 I tell you most solemnly, (C2)
   whoever listens to my words,
   and believes in the one who sent me, (C1)
   has eternal life;
   without being brought to judgment
   he has passed from death to life.
25 I tell you most solemnly,
   the hour will come—in fact it is here already—
   when the dead will hear the voice of the Son of God,
   and all who hear it will live.
26 For the Father, who is the source of life,
   has made the Son the source of life;
27 and, because he is the Son of Man,
   has appointed him supreme judge.
28 Do not be surprised at this,
   for the hour is coming
   when the dead will leave their graves
   at the sound of his voice:
29 those who did good (C3)
   will rise again to life; (C2)
   and those who did evil, to condemnation.
30 I can do nothing by myself,
   I can only judge as I am told to judge,
   and my judging is just,
   because my aim is to do not my own will,
   but the will of him who sent me.

31 "Were I to testify on my own behalf,
   my testimony would not be valid;
32 but there is another witness who can speak on my behalf,
   and I know that his testimony is valid.
33 You sent messengers to John,
   and he gave his testimony to the truth: (C3)

34 not that I depend on human testimony;
no, it is for your salvation that I speak of this.
35 John was a lamp alight and shining (C3)
and for a time you were content to enjoy the light that he gave.
36 But my testimony is greater than John's:
the works my Father has given me to carry out,
these same works of mine
testify that the Father has sent me.
37 Besides, the Father who sent me
bears witness to me himself.
You have never heard his voice,
you have never seen his shape,
38 and his word finds no home in you
because you do not believe (C2)
in the one he has sent.

39 "You study the scriptures,
believing that in them you have eternal life; (C1)
now these same scriptures testify to me,
40 and yet you refuse to come to me for life! (C2)
41 As for human approval, this means nothing to me.
42 Besides, I know you too well:
you have no love of God in you. (C2)
43 I have come in the name of my Father
and you refuse to accept me; (C2)
if someone else comes in his own name
you will accept him. (C2)

JOHN

44 How can you believe, (C1)
since you look to one another for approval (C2)
and are not concerned
with the approval that comes from the one God?
45 Do not imagine that I am going to accuse you before the Father:
you place your hopes on Moses,
and Moses will be your accuser.
46 If you really believed him (C1)
you would believe me too,
since it was I that he was writing about;
47 but if you refuse to believe what he wrote, (C2)
how can you believe what I say?" (C1)

Week 1 Day 4
Four C's Meditations
on St. John 5:1-47

1. In today's meditation, blessed Lord, we read of the man You miraculously healed who had been sick for thirty-eight years. We learned also that this illness was due to his own sinfulness. "Now that you are well again, be sure not to sin anymore, or something worse may happen to you."*(28)*

2. Lord, we were impressed by the fact that you loved this man in spite of his sinfulness. This gives us comfort, since we are confident that You love us, too, who are also sinners. But that does not mean that You are willing to overlook our sinful ways. Not at all, since You want us to be free of sin so we can be fit members of Your heavenly Kingdom.

3. In Heaven there is no room for sin. Therefore, You became man and sacrificed Yourself on the Cross for us, so that we could have our sins not only forgiven, but removed through the cleansing action of Your powerful grace.

4. Lord, inspire us daily to examine our consciences and confess our sins so that we can receive Your forgiveness and grace, and become ever more ready to enter the fullness of Your holy Kingdom.

5. Jesus, while meditating on the account of Your miraculous healing, our attention focused on the fact that sin can be an occasion for illness. This is worth thinking about because today this is often forgotten or denied. Of course, Lord, some illnesses have nothing to do with personal sin as You Yourself testified with respect to a man born blind.

6. "'Rabbi, who sinned, this man or his parents, for him to have been born blind?' 'Neither he nor his parents sinned,' Jesus answered, 'he was born blind so that the works of God might be displayed in him.'"*(29)*

7. With respect to sin-caused illnesses, we think of people who refuse to take proper care of themselves and thus become ill; abusers of alcohol and drugs, for example. We are learning also of the harm done to infants in the womb from venereal diseases and from the drug and alcohol abuse of their parents. Moreover, it has been long known that lack of charity between parents can cause psychological damage to both the parents themselves and to their children.

8. Jesus, Divine Physician, cleanse our hearts of all sinful tendencies since they poison the soul and may also lead to physical and psychological illnesses. May we always be open to receiving Your healing grace within our hearts.

9. Also Lord, never let us forget that there are many victim souls who are uniting their sickness and suffering with Your sacrifice on the Cross and are therefore gaining great merit to atone for the sins of the world.

10. Jesus, Our Lord, in our lesson for today, You are quoted as saying that whoever listens to Your words and believes, i.e. has faith, in the Father has eternal life.(30) This, of course, is true, but it is not the entire story as we learn from other portions of Scripture. The supernatural gift of faith does give us access to eternal life or salvation, but Baptism is also necessary. And the supernatural gift of seed-charity is required, as well, if we are to retain and strengthen our participation in eternal life. In other words,

when we examine Scripture as a whole, we see that You are teaching us that we do not receive salvation by faith alone, but by faith in conjunction with Baptism and seed-charity.

11. The following passages demonstrate this truth.

12. "Hearing this, they were cut to the heart and said to Peter and the apostles, 'What must we do, brothers (to be saved)?' 'You must repent,' Peter answered, 'and eveyone of you must be baptized in the name of Jesus Christ for the forgiveness of your sins and you will receive the gift of the Holy Spirit.'"(31)

13. "I tell you most solemnly, unless a man is born through water and the Spirit (Baptism), he cannot enter the kingdom of God."(32)

14. "Take the case, my brothers, of someone who had never done a single good (charitable) act but claims that he has faith. Will that faith save him?.... If good works do not go with it, it is quite dead.... A body dies when it is separated from good deeds."(33)

15. "Christians are told by the Spirit to look to faith for those rewards that righteousness hopes for, since in Christ Jesus...what matters is faith that expresses itself in love."(34)

16. Finally, there is that passage, Lord, in which St. John notes that there is such a thing as deadly, grave or mortal sin. That is, a sin which causes even a believing Christian to be cut-off from eternal life, since by committing it he becomes spiritually dead. *(For a discussion of mortal sin, see "The Catholic Catechism," pp. 183-185.)*

17. "If anybody sees his brother committing a sin that is not a deadly sin, he has only to pray, and God will give life to the sinner - not those who commit a deadly sin; for there is a sin, that is death and I will not say that you must pray about that. Every kind of wrongdoing is sin, but not all sin is deadly."(35)

18. Heavenly Father, You have told us that whatever we do without seed-charity is worth nothing.(36) Send Your Holy Spirit to pour into our hearts the precious gift of seed-charity without which anyone who is alive is regarded as spiritually dead in Your sight. Grant this for the sake of Your only Son, Jesus Christ. Amen.

Try to read these Scripture passages and meditations in a reflective manner every day. The Holy Spirit will reveal more insights to you each time you do so.

Please read and meditate on Chapter II, Paragraphs 1 to 6 of Peaceful Seed Living, Volume I.

**WEEK 1 DAY 5
The Gospel of St. John
Chapters 6:1-7:52**

IV. ANOTHER PASSOVER, THE BREAD OF LIFE

The miracle of the loaves

6 1 Some time after this, Jesus went off to the other side of the Sea of Galilee—or of 2 Tiberias—·and a large crowd followed him, impressed by the signs he gave by curing the 3 sick. ·Jesus climbed the hillside, and sat 4 down there with his disciples. ·It was shortly before the Jewish feast of Passover.

5 Looking up, Jesus saw the crowds approaching and said to Philip, "Where can we buy some bread for these people to eat?" 6 He only said this to test Philip; he himself 7 knew exactly what he was going to do. ·Philip answered, "Two hundred denarii would only buy enough to give them a small piece each." 8 One of his disciples, Andrew, Simon Peter's 9 brother, said, ·"There is a small boy here with five barley loaves and two fish; but what

JOHN

10 is that between so many?" ·Jesus said to them, "Make the people sit down." There was plenty of grass there, and as many as five
11 thousand men sat down. ·Then Jesus took the loaves, gave thanks, and gave them out to all who were sitting ready; he then did the same with the fish, giving out as much as was
12 wanted. ·When they had eaten enough he said to the disciples, "Pick up the pieces left over,
13 so that nothing gets wasted." ·So they picked them up, and filled twelve hampers with scraps left over from the meal of five barley
14 loaves. ·The people, seeing this sign that he had given, said, "This really is the prophet (c1)
15 who is to come into the world." ·Jesus, who could see they were about to come and take him by force and make him king, escaped back to the hills by himself.

Jesus walks on the waters

16 That evening the disciples went down to
17 the shore of the lake and ·got into a boat to make for Capernaum on the other side of the lake. It was getting dark by now and Jesus
18 had still not rejoined them. ·The wind was
19 strong, and the sea was getting rough. ·They had rowed three or four miles when they saw Jesus walking on the lake and coming to-
20 wards the boat. This frightened them, ·but he
21 said, "It is I. Do not be afraid." ·They were for taking him into the boat, but in no time it reached the shore at the place they were making for.

The discourse in the synagogue at Capernaum

22 Next day, the crowd that had stayed on the other side saw that only one boat had been there, and that Jesus had not got into the boat with his disciples, but that the disciples had
23 set off by themselves. ·Other boats, however, had put in from Tiberias, near the place

24 where the bread had been eaten. ·When the people saw that neither Jesus nor his disciples were there, they got into those boats and crossed to Capernaum to look for Jesus.
25 When they found him on the other side, they said to him, "Rabbi, when did you come
26 here?" ·Jesus answered:

"I tell you most solemnly,
you are not looking for me
because you have seen the signs
but because you had all the bread you wanted to eat.
27 Do not work for food that cannot last,
but work for food that endures to eternal life, (c3)
the kind of food the Son of Man is offering you,
for on him the Father, God himself, has set his seal."

28 Then they said to him, "What must we do if we are to do the works that God wants?"
29 Jesus gave them this answer, "This is work- (c1) ing for God: you must believe in the one he
30 has sent." ·So they said, "What sign will you give to show us that we should believe in (c1)
31 you? What work will you do? ·Our fathers had manna to eat in the desert; as scripture says: *He gave them bread from heaven to eat.*"[a]

60

32 Jesus answered:

"I tell you most solemnly,
it was not Moses who gave you bread from heaven,
it is my Father who gives you the bread from heaven,
the true bread;
33 for the bread of God
is that which comes down from heaven
and gives life to the world."

34 "Sir," they said, "give us that bread al-
35 ways." ·Jesus answered:

"I am the bread of life.
He who comes to me will never be hungry; (C3)
he who believes in me will never thirst. (C1)
36 But, as I have told you,
you can see me and still you do not believe. (C2)
37 All that the Father gives me will come to me, (C3)
and whoever comes to me
I shall not turn him away; (C3)
38 because I have come from heaven,
not to do my own will,
but to do the will of the one who sent me.
39 Now the will of him who sent me
is that I should lose nothing
of all that he has given to me,
and that I should raise it up on the last day.

61

JOHN

40 Yes, it is my Father's will
that whoever sees the Son and believes in (C1)
him
shall have eternal life,
and that I shall raise him up on the last day."
41 Meanwhile the Jews were complaining to each other about him, because he had said, "I am the bread that came down from
42 heaven." •"Surely this is Jesus son of Joseph," they said. "We know his father and mother. How can he now say, 'I have come
43 down from heaven'?" •Jesus said in reply, "Stop complaining to each other. (C2)

(C1)
44 "No one can come to me (C3)
unless he is drawn by the Father who sent me,
and I will raise him up at the last day.
45 It is written in the prophets:
They will all be taught by God,[b]
and to hear the teaching of the Father,
and learn from it,
is to come to me.
46 Not that anybody has seen the Father,
except the one who comes from God:
he has seen the Father.
47 I tell you most solemnly, (C1)
everybody who believes has eternal life.
48 I am the bread of life.
49 Your fathers ate the manna in the desert
and they are dead;
50 but this is the bread that comes down from heaven,
so that a man may eat it and not die. (C3)
51 I am the living bread which has come down (C1)
from heaven.
Anyone who eats this bread will live for (C3)
ever;
and the bread that I shall give
is my flesh, for the life of the world."

JOHN

52 Then the Jews started arguing with one another: "How can this man give us his flesh
53 to eat?" they said. ·Jesus replied:

"I tell you most solemnly,
if you do not eat the flesh of the Son of Man (c2)
and drink his blood,
you will not have life in you.
54 Anyone who does eat my flesh and drink my blood
has eternal life, (c3)
and I shall raise him up on the last day.
55 For my flesh is real food
and my blood is real drink.
56 He who eats my flesh and drinks my blood (c3)
lives in me
and I live in him.
57 As I, who am sent by the living Father,
myself draw life from the Father,
so whoever eats me will draw life from (c3)
me.
58 This is the bread come down from heaven;
not like the bread our ancestors ate:
they are dead,
but anyone who eats this bread will live for (c3)
ever."

59 He taught this doctrine at Capernaum, in
60 the synagogue. ·After hearing it, many of his followers said, "This is intolerable language.
61 How could anyone accept it?" ·Jesus was aware that his followers were complaining about it and said, "Does this upset you?
62 What if you should see the Son of Man ascend to where he was before?

63 "It is the spirit that gives life,
the flesh has nothing to offer.
The words I have spoken to you are spirit
and they are life.

64 "But there are some of you who do not (c2)
believe." For Jesus knew from the outset
those who did not believe, and who it was (c2)

65 that would betray him. •He went on, "This is why I told you that no one could come to
66 me unless the Father allows him." •After this, many of his disciples left him and stopped going with him. (C2)

Peter's profession of faith

67 Then Jesus said to the Twelve, "What about you, do you want to go away too?"
68 Simon Peter answered, "Lord, who shall we go to? You have the message of eternal life,
69 and we believe; we know that you are the (C1)
70 Holy One of God." •Jesus replied, "Have I not chosen you, you Twelve? Yet one of you (C2)
71 is a devil." •He meant Judas son of Simon Iscariot, since this was the man, one of the Twelve, who was going to betray him. (C2)

V. THE FEAST OF TABERNACLES

Jesus goes up to Jerusalem for the feast and teaches there

1 7 After this Jesus stayed in Galilee; he could not stay in Judaea, because the Jews were out to kill him. (C2)
2 As the Jewish feat of Tabernacles drew
3 near, •his brothers*a* said to him, "Why not leave this place and go to Judaea, and let your
4 disciples*b* see the works you are doing; •if a man wants to be known he does not do things in secret; since you are doing all this, you

5 should let the whole world see." ·Not even
6 his brothers, in fact, had faith in him. ·Jesus (c2)
answered, "The right time for me has not
come yet, but any time is the right time for
7 you. ·The world cannot hate you, but it does (c2)
hate me, because I give evidence that its ways
8 are evil. ·Go up to the festival yourselves: I
am not going to this festival, because for me
9 the time is not ripe yet." ·Having said that,
he stayed behind in Galilee.
10   However, after his brothers had left for the
festival, he went up as well, but quite privately, without drawing attention to himself.
11 At the festival the Jews were on the look-out
12 for him: "Where is he?" they said. ·People
stood in groups whispering^c about him. Some
said, "He is a good man"; others, "No, he (c2)
13 is leading the people astray." ·Yet no one
spoke about him openly, for fear of the Jews.
14   When the festival was half over, Jesus
15 went to the Temple and began to teach. ·The
Jews were astonished and said, "How did he
16 learn to read? He has not been taught." ·Jesus
answered them:

"My teaching is not from myself: (c1)
it comes from the one who sent me;
17 and if anyone is prepared to do his will, (c3)
he will know whether my teaching is from God
or whether my doctrine is my own.

JOHN

18 When a man's doctrine is his own
he is hoping to get honor for himself;
but when he is working for the honor of one
who sent him,
then he is sincere
and by no means an impostor.
19 Did not Moses give you the Law?
And yet not one of you keeps the Law! (C2)

20 "Why do you want to kill me?" ·The crowd (C2)
replied, "You are mad! Who wants to kill
21 you?" ·Jesus answered, "One work I did, and
22 you are all surprised by it. ·Moses ordered
you to practice circumcision—not that it began with him, it goes back to the patriarchs
23 —and you circumcise on the sabbath. ·Now
if a man can be circumcised on the sabbath
so that the Law of Moses is not broken, why
are you angry with me for making a man (C2)
24 whole and complete on the sabbath? ·Do
not keep judging according to appearances;
let your judgment be according to what is
right."

The people discuss the origin of the Messiah

25 Meanwhile some of the people of Jerusalem were saying, "Isn't this the man they (C2)
26 want to kill? ·And here he is, speaking freely,
and they have nothing to say to him! Can it
be true the authorities have made up their
27 minds that he is the Christ? ·Yet we all know
where he comes from, but when the Christ
appears no one will know where he comes
from."[d]
28 Then, as Jesus taught in the Temple, he
cried out:

"Yes, you know me and you know where I
came from.
Yet I have not come of myself:
no, there is one who sent me and I really
come from him,
and you do not know him, (C2)

JOHN

29 but I know him
because I have come from him
and it was he who sent me."

30 They would have arrested him then, but because his time had not yet come no one laid a hand on him. (C2)

Jesus foretells his approaching departure

31 There were many people in the crowds, however, who believed in him; they were saying, "When the Christ comes, will he give (C1)
32 more signs than this man?" ·Hearing that rumors like this about him were spreading among the people, the Pharisees sent the Temple police to arrest him.
33 Then Jesus said: (C2)

"I shall remain with you for only a short time now;
then I shall go back to the one who sent me.
34 You will look for me and will not find me:
where I am
you cannot come."

35 The Jews then said to one another, "Where is he going that we shan't be able to find him? Is he going abroad to the people who are dispersed among the Greeks and will he
36 teach the Greeks? ·What does he mean when he says:

'You will look for me and will not find me:
where I am,
you cannot come?'"

The promise of living water

37 On the last day and greatest day of the festival, Jesus stood there and cried out:

---

d. Although the prophecy that the Messiah would be born in Bethlehem was well known, it was commonly believed that he would appear suddenly from some secret place.

"If any man is thirsty, let him come to me!
38 Let the man come and drink •who believes (c1)
in me!"

As scripture says: From his breast shall flow fountains of living water.*e*

39 He was speaking of the Spirit which those (c1) who believed in him were to receive; for there was no Spirit as yet because Jesus had not yet been glorified.

Fresh discussions on the origin of the Messiah

40 Several people who had been listening
41 said, "Surely he must be the prophet," •and (c1) some said, "He is the Christ," but others said, "Would the Christ be from Galilee?
42 Does not scripture say that the Christ must be descended from David and come from the
43 town of Bethlehem?" •So the people could
44 not agree about him. •Some would have liked to arrest him, but no one actually laid hands (c2) on him.

45 The police went back to the chief priests and Pharisees who said to them, "Why
46 haven't you brought him?" •The police replied, "There has never been anybody who
47 has spoken like him." •"So," the Pharisees answered, "you have been led astray as well?
48 Have any of the authorities believed in him?
49 Any of the Pharisees? •This rabble knows (c2) nothing about the Law—they are damned."
50 One of them, Nicodemus—the same man who had come to Jesus earlier—said to them,
51 "But surely the Law does not allow us to pass judgment on a man without giving him a hear-
52 ing and discovering what he is about?" •To this they answered, "Are you a Galilean too? Go into the matter, and see for yourself: prophets do not come out of Galilee."

e. Life-giving water for Zion was a theme of the readings from scripture on the feast of Tabernacles (Zc 14:8, Ezk 47:13f); the liturgy included prayers for rain and the commemoration of the miracle of Moses and the water, Ex 17. **f.** The author of this passage, 7:53-8:11, is not John; the oldest MSS do not include it or place it elsewhere. The style is that of the Synoptics.

**Week 1 Day 5
Four C's Meditations
on St. John 6:1-7:52**

1. Jesus, today's Scripture reading stressed the fact that You are the Bread of Life which we must consume if we are to enjoy the supernatural or divine life of the Kingdom of God. As the Bread of Life Who comes down from Heaven to give us this life You demonstrate once more Your immense love for us.

2. "I am the bread of life. Your fathers ate manna in the desert and they are dead; but this is the bread that comes down from heaven, so that a man may eat it and not die...and the bread I shall give is my flesh, for the life of the world....

3. "I tell you most solemnly, if you do not eat the flesh of the Son of Man and drink his blood, you will not have life in you. Anyone who does eat my flesh and drink my blood has eternal life, and I shall raise him up on the last

day. For my flesh is real food and my blood is real drink. He who eats my flesh and drinks my blood lives in me and I live in him." *(37)*

4. The Catholic Church holds that Your teaching about the Bread of Life is a direct reference to the Holy Eucharist in which You continually nourish Your faithful followers with Your Body and Blood. *(See "The Catholic Catechism," for an explanation of the Eucharist, pp. 456-481.)*

5. Most Sacred and Eucharistic Heart of Jesus, help us to always venerate You as the Bread of Life which You give to nourish our souls and preserve us in Your friendship.

6. Unfortunately, over the centuries there have been some who have denied that You were the Bread of Life in the setting of the Holy Eucharist. Consequently, strengthen our faith in this regard so that we may truly believe the unbroken tradition from the earliest days of Christianity that at the Last Supper You caused bread to become Your Body, which is the Bread of life, and You caused the cup of wine to become Your sacrificial Blood.

7. Since it is not self-evident that You are the Bread of Life in the Eucharist, we must rely on Your words with the aid of Your gift of faith. For without faith this great mystery could never be accepted.

8. Jesus, even some of Your disciples had no faith in this regard as we learned in today's reading.

9. "'But there are some of you who do not believe.... This is why I told you that no one can come to me unless the Father allows him.'" After this, many of his disciples left him and stopped going with him."

10. "Then Jesus said to the Twelve, 'What about you, do you want to go away too?' Simon Peter answered, 'Lord, who shall we go to? You have the message of eternal life, and we believe.'"*(38)*

11. Our Savior, give us a steadfast faith in You as the Bread of Life present in the Holy Eucharist. And may those who receive You there allow You to nourish their souls.

12. Next, Lord, our attention dwelt on St. John's account of Your attendance at the Jewish Feast of the Tabernacles in Jerusalem. While there You cried out:

13. "If any man is thirsty, let him come to me! Let the man come and drink who believes in me."*(39)*

14. Then St. John went on to say:

15. "He was speaking of the Spirit which those who believed in him were to receive; for there was no Spirit yet because Jesus had not yet been glorified."*(40)*

16. First, Lord, You told us that You want to feed us with Your Sacred Body and Blood. Now, You tell us that through You we can also receive the life-giving Holy Spirit, Who is symbolized as living water. Yes, Jesus, through the outpouring of Your Sacred Heart

we receive God the Holy Spirit, Who gives us the supernatural gifts we need to lead a holy life, a life that imitates Yours. If we allow the Holy Spirit to remain within our hearts we shall never again experience spiritual death. Therefore, our souls will be constantly refreshed and invigorated, more so than when a thirsty person is refreshed and invigorated by drinking fresh spring water.

17. "Whoever drinks this water will get thirsty again; but anyone who drinks the water I shall give will never be thirsty again: the water I shall give will turn into a spring inside him, welling up to eternal life."(41)

18. Lord, You have made our bodies temples of God the Holy Spirit. May our lives be such that He is always present within these temples, refreshing and invigorating our souls, and preparing us for a life with You and the Father in eternity. Amen.

Try to read these Scripture passages and meditations in a reflective manner every day. The Holy Spirit will reveal more insights to you each time you do so.

Please read and meditate on Chapter II, Paragraphs 7 to 15 of Peaceful Seed Living, Volume I.

WEEK 1 DAY 6
The Gospel of St. John
Chapter 8:1-59

The adulterous woman *ƒ*

1 They all went home, 8 and Jesus went to the Mount of Olives.
2 At daybreak he appeared in the Temple again; and as all the people came to him, he sat down and began to teach them.
3 The scribes and Pharisees brought a woman along who had been caught committing adultery; and making her stand there in
4 full view of everybody, ·they said to Jesus, "Master, this woman was caught in the very
5 act of committing adultery, ·and Moses has ordered us in the Law to condemn women like this to death by stoning. What have you
6 to say?" ·They asked him this as a test, looking for something to use against him. But Jesus bent down and started writing on the
7 ground with his finger. ·As they persisted with their question, he looked up and said, "If there is one of you who has not sinned, let him be the first to throw a stone at her."
8 Then he bent down and wrote on the ground
9 again. ·When they heard this they went away one by one, beginning with the eldest, until Jesus was left alone with the woman, who

10 remained standing there. ·He looked up and said, "Woman, where are they? Has no one
11 condemned you?" ·"No one, sir," she replied. "Neither do I condemn you," said Jesus; "go away, and don't sin any more." (C2)

Jesus, the light of the world

12 When Jesus spoke to the people again, he said:

"I am the light of the world;
anyone who follows me will not be walking (C3)
  in the dark;
he will have the light of life."

A discussion on the testimony of Jesus to himself

13 At this the Pharisees said to him, "You are testifying on your own behalf; your testimony (C2)
14 is not valid." ·Jesus replied:

"It is true that I am testifying on my own behalf,
but my testimony is still valid,
because I know
where I came from and where I am going;
but you do not know
where I come from or where I am going.
15 You judge by human standards; (C2)
I judge no one,
16 but if I judge,
my judgment will be sound,
because I am not alone:
the one who sent me is with me;
17 and in your Law it is written
that the testimony of two witnesses is valid.
18 I may be testifying on my own behalf,
but the Father who sent me is my witness too."

19 They asked him, "Where is your Father?" Jesus answered:

"You do not know me, nor do you know my Father;

JOHN

if you did know me, you would know my Father as well."

20 He spoke these words in the Treasury, while teaching in the Temple. No one arrested him, because his time had not yet come.

The unbelieving Jews warned

21 Again he said to them:

"I am going away; you will look for me (C2)
and you will die in your sin.
Where I am going, you cannot come."

22 The Jews said to one another, "Will he kill himself? Is that what he means by saying, 'Where I am going, you cannot come'?"
23 Jesus went on:

"You are from below;
I am from above.
You are of this world;
I am not of this world.
24 I have told you already: You will die in your (C2)
sins.
Yes, if you do not believe that I am He, (C2)
you will die in your sins."

25 So they said to him, "Who are you?" Jesus answered:

"What I have told you from the outset.
26 About you I have much to say
and much to condemn; (C2)
but the one who sent me is truthful,
and what I have learned from him
I declared to the world."

27 They failed to understand that he was
28 talking to them about the Father. ·So Jesus said:

"When you have lifted up the Son of Man,
then you will know that I am He

75

and that I do nothing of myself:
what the Father has taught me
is what I preach;
29 he who sent me is with me,
and has not left me to myself,
for I always do what pleases him."

30 As he was saying this, many came to believe in him. (C1)

Jesus and Abraham

31 To the Jews who believed in him Jesus said: (C1)

"If you make my word your home
you will indeed be my disciples, (C3)
32 you will learn the truth
and the truth will make you free."

33 They answered, "We are descended from Abraham and we have never been the slaves of anyone; what do you mean, 'You will be
34 made free'?" ·Jesus replied:

"I tell you most solemnly,
everyone who commits sin is a slave. (C2)
35 Now the slave's place in the house is not assured,
but the son's place is assured.
36 So if the Son makes you free,
you will be free indeed.

37 I know that you are descended from Abraham;
but in spite of that you want to kill me
because nothing I say has penetrated into you. (C2)
38 What I, for my part, speak of
is what I have seen with my Father;
but you, you put into action
the lessons learned from your father."

39 They repeated, "Our father is Abraham." Jesus said to them:

"If you were Abraham's children,
you would do as Abraham did.
40 As it is, you want to kill me (C2)
when I tell you the truth
as I have learned it from God;
that is not what Abraham did.
41 What you are doing is what your father does."

"We were not born of prostitution,"[a] they (C2)
42 went on; "we have one father: God." ·Jesus answered:

"If God were your father, you would love me, (C3)

---

8 a. By "prostitution" the prophets often mean religious infidelity, cf. Ho 1:2.

JOHN

since I have come here from God; yes, I have come from him;
not that I came because I chose,
no, I was sent, and by him.
43 Do you know why you cannot take in what I say?
It is because you are unable to understand my language.
44 The devil is your father,
and you prefer to do (C2)
what your father wants.

He was a murderer from the start; (C2)
he was never grounded in the truth;
there is no truth in him at all:
when he lies (C2)
he is drawing on his own store,
because he is a liar, and the father of lies.
45 But as for me, I speak the truth
and for that very reason,
you do not believe me. (C2)
46 Can one of you convict me of sin?
If I speak the truth, why do you not believe (C2)
me?
47 A child of God (C1)
listens to the words of God; (C3)
if you refuse to listen, (C2)
it is because you are not God's children."

48 The Jews replied, "Are we not right in (C2) saying that you are a Samaritan and possessed by a devil?" Jesus answered:

49 "I am not possessed;
no, I honor my Father,
but you want to dishonor me. (C2)
50 Not that I care for my own glory,
there is someone who takes care of that and is the judge of it.
51 I tell you most solemnly,
whoever keeps my word (C3)
will never see death."

52 The Jews said, "Now we know for certain that you are possessed. Abraham is dead, and (c2) the prophets are dead, and yet you say, 'Whoever keeps my word will never know the taste
53 of death.' ·Are you greater than our father Abraham, who is dead? The prophets are dead too. Who are you claiming to be?"
54 Jesus answered:

"If I were to seek my own glory
that would be no glory at all;
my glory is conferred by the Father,
by the one of whom you say, 'He is our God'
55 although you do not know him. (c2)
But I know him,
and if I were to say: I do not know him,
I should be a liar, as you are liars yourselves. (c2)
But I do know him, and I faithfully keep his word.
56 Your father Abraham rejoiced
to think that he would see my Day; (c3)
he saw it and was glad."

57 The Jews then said, "You are not fifty yet,
58 and you have seen Abraham!" ·Jesus replied:

"I tell you most solemnly,
before Abraham ever was,
I Am."

59 At this they picked up stones to throw at him;[b] but Jesus hid himself and left the Tem- (c2) ple.

79

Week 1 Day 6
Four C's Meditations
on St. John 8:1-59

1. Today, Lord, our scriptural reading included the well-known account of the adulteress who faced death by stoning. In this situation we learned a valuable lesson about fallen human nature.

2. There is a tendency in all of us to overlook our own sins by pointing to the sins of others, and the action of the Scribes and Pharisees in this account illustrates this truth. Lord, You reminded them of their own sinfulness when they, with zealous self-righteousness, wished to put the adulterous woman to death.

3. Perhaps, none of the Scribes and Pharisees ever committed adultery, but they, the religious leaders of their day, were prone to hypocrisy as You time and again pointed out to them.

4. "Alas for you, scribes and Pharisees, you hypocrites! You who pay your tithe of mint and dill and cummin and have neglected the weightier matters of the Law-justice, mercy, good faith! These you should have practiced, without neglecting the others. You blind guides! Straining out gnats and swallowing camels."*(42)*

5. Surely, Lord, as serious as adultery is, the injustice, the lack of mercy, and the lack of good faith which the religious leaders committed were very grave as well. And the

hypocrisy surrounding these sins was even worse.

6. We noticed too, Jesus, that You Who had no sin, and therefore could condemn the adulteress without hypocrisy, refused to do so. Presumably, knowing her inner thoughts, You realized that, unlike the Scribes and Pharisees, she was sincerely repentant and ashamed of her transgression of the moral law. Consequently, You simply dismissed her with a warning not to sin again.

7. Most Sacred Heart of Jesus, guard us against the grievous sin of hypocrisy. May we always be more concerned with ridding ourselves of our own sins than we are of dwelling on the sinfulness of others.

8. Jesus, in today's meditation You also told Your listeners that they could not follow You because they belonged to this world.*(43)* And elsewhere You said to Your Apostles:

9. "If the world hates you, remember that it hated me before you. If you belonged to the world, the world would love you as its own; but because you do not belong to the world, because my choice withdrew you from the world, therefore the world hates you."*(44)*

10. Jesus, some might think that You were implying the material universe was evil, and therefore it must be avoided as much as possible. But, of course, this is not what You meant. The material world, and the spiritual world for that matter, cannot be evil in themselves because You created them and

continually keep them in existence. What You really had reference to were certain rational elements of creation, namely, the "world" of Your human and angelic (demonic) beings, divorced from Your divine friendship. It was this "world," that You had in mind, over which satan, the "prince of this world," ruled and will continue to rule till the end of time.*(45)*

11. The term "flesh" is also used at times in Scripture in a similar manner to "world." When it is used in this way it has reference to individual human bodies which are not governed by the Holy Spirit, but by sin. Flesh used in this manner, then, does not mean that flesh as such is evil. Indeed, it cannot be because You made it.

12. Dearest Jesus, always protect us against the temptations of the world, the flesh and the devil so that we may always enjoy Your presence and experience the peace of God which surpasses all understanding.

13. Finally, Lord, we noticed in today's reading the contrasting terms "truth" and "lie."*(46)* First, You spoke of Your words as conveying the truth, truth which will make us free. Then You spoke of satan as the father of lies whom some of the leaders of the Jews turned to as their spiritual father.*(47)*

14. Yes, Lord, Your words are true and they lead to eternal life.

15. How do we know they are true? Among other things, the sanctity of Your life, attested to by Your holy followers, supports the truthfulness of Your words. And the numerous miracles You performed while on earth, witnessed by Your disciples, also bear witness to Your veracity. And so do the thousands of miracles performed in your Name over the centuries by Your faithful followers. But, especially the miracle of Your Resurrection from the dead points to the truth of Your teaching.

16. Jesus, the words that You taught are indeed true. And as You said, they will make us free from the powers of sin and death, if we believe them and put them into practice. Please, Lord, strengthen our faith in You and in Your words of eternal life.

17. In glaring contrast to You Who are the Truth, there exists satan, the father of lies, as You called him.*(48)* He would do anything in his power to have us reject You, Jesus, and subscribe to his lies which lead to eternal destruction. Consequently, we must never cease believing Your words by means of the supernatural gift of faith.

18. St. Peter also, Lord, as You know, warned us about satan. And he pointed out that we will defeat satan by remaining strong in faith.

19. "Be calm but vigilant, because your enemy the devil is prowling round like a roaring lion, looking for someone to eat. Stand up to him, strong in faith...."*(49)*

20. Lord, Jesus, we humbly ask You to protect us against the snares and wiles of the devil and his fellow demons. And may we always cling to You Who are the Way, the Truth and the Life. Amen.

Try to re-read and meditate on these Scripture passages and reflections at least one more time today.

Please read and meditate on Chapter II, Paragraphs 16 to 31 of Peaceful Seed Living, Volume I.

WEEK 1 DAY 7
The Gospel of St. John
Chapter 9:1-11:57

The cure of the man born blind

9 ¹ As he went along, he saw a man who had ² been blind from birth. ·His disciples asked him, "Rabbi, who sinned, this man or his (C2) parents, for him to have been born blind?" (C3) ³ "Neither he nor his parents sinned," Jesus answered. "He was born blind so that the works of God might be displayed in him.

⁴ "As long as the day lasts
I must carry out the work of the one who sent me;
the night will soon be here when no one can work.
⁵ As long as I am in the world
I am the light of the world."

⁶ Having said this, he spat on the ground, made a paste with the spittle, put this over ⁷ the eyes of the blind man, ·and said to him, "Go and wash in the Pool of Siloam"^a (a name that means "sent"). So the blind man went off and washed himself, and came away with his sight restored.

8 His neighbors and people who earlier had seen him begging said, "Isn't this the man
9 who used to sit and beg?" ·Some said, "Yes, it is the same one." Others said, "No, he only looks like him." The man himself said, "I am
10 the man." ·So they said to him, "Then how
11 do your eyes come to be open?" ·"The man called Jesus," he answered, "made a paste, daubed my eyes with it and said to me, 'Go and wash at Siloam;' so I went, and when I
12 washed I could see." ·They asked, "Where is he?" "I don't know," he answered.

13 They brought the man who had been blind
14 to the Pharisees. ·It had been a sabbath day when Jesus made the paste and opened the
15 man's eyes, ·so when the Pharisees asked him how he had come to see, he said, "He put a paste on my eyes, and I washed, and
16 I can see." ·Then some of the Pharisees said, "This man cannot be from God: he does not keep the sabbath." Others said, "How could a sinner produce signs like this?" And there
17 was disagreement among them. ·So they spoke to the blind man again, "What have you to say about him yourself, now that he has opened your eyes?" "He is a prophet" replied the man.

18 However, the Jews would not believe that the man had been blind and had gained his sight, without first sending for his parents and
19 asking them, "Is this man really your son who you say was born blind? If so, how is
20 it that he is now able to see?" ·His parents answered, "We know he is our son and we
21 know he was born blind, ·but we don't know how it is that he can see now, or who opened his eyes. He is old enough: let him speak for
22 himself." ·His parents spoke like this out of fear of the Jews, who had already agreed to expel from the synagogue anyone who should acknowledge Jesus as the Christ. (C2)

---

b. Stoning was the penalty for blasphemy. Cf. 10:33.
9 a. Water from this pool was drawn during the feast of Tabernacles to symbolize the waters of blessing.

JOHN

23 This was why his parents said, "He is old enough; ask him."

24 So the Jews again sent for the man and said to him, "Give glory to God!*b* For our part, 25 we know that this man is a sinner." ·The man answered, "I don't know if he is a sinner; I only know that I was blind and now I can 26 see." ·They said to him, "What did he do to 27 you? How did he open your eyes?" ·He replied, "I have told you once and you wouldn't listen. Why do you want to hear it all again? Do you want to become his disciples too?" 28 At this they hurled abuse at him: "You can be his disciple," they said; "we are disciples 29 of Moses: ·we know that God spoke to Moses, but as for this man, we don't know 30 where he comes from." ·The man replied, "Now here is an astonishing thing! He has opened my eyes, and you don't know where 31 he comes from! ·We know that God doesn't listen to sinners, but God does listen to men 32 who are devout and do his will. ·Ever since the world began it is unheard of for anyone to open the eyes of a man who was born 33 blind; ·if this man were not from God, he 34 couldn't do a thing." ·"Are you trying to teach us," they replied, "and you a sinner through and through, since you were born!" And they drove him away.

35 Jesus heard they had driven him away, and when he found him he said to him, "Do you 36 believe in the Son of Man?" ·"Sir," the man replied, "tell me who he is so that I may 37 believe in him." ·Jesus said, "You are 38 looking at him: he is speaking to you." ·The man said, "Lord, I believe," and worshiped him.

---

b. I.e., putting the man on oath.

39 Jesus said: (C3)

> "It is for judgment
> that I have come into this world,
> so that those without sight may see
> and those with sight turn blind."

40 Hearing this, some Pharisees who were present said to him, "We are not blind, surely?"
41 Jesus replied:

> "Blind? If you were,
> you would not be guilty,
> but since you say, 'We see,'
> your guilt remains. (C2)

The good shepherd

1 **10** "I tell you most solemnly, anyone who does not enter the sheepfold through the gate, but gets in some other way is a thief (C2)
2 and a brigand. ·The one who enters through (C3)
3 the gate is the shepherd of the flock; ·the gatekeeper lets him in, the sheep hear his voice, one by one he calls his own sheep and (C3)
4 leads them out. ·When he has brought out his flock, he goes ahead of them, and the sheep fol- (C3)
5 low because they know his voice. ·They never follow a stranger but run away from him: (C3) they do not recognize the voice of strangers."
6 Jesus told them*a* this parable but they failed to understand what he meant by telling it to them.
7 So Jesus spoke to them again:

88

"I tell you most solemnly,
I am the gate of the sheepfold.
8 All others who have come
are thieves and brigands; (C2)
but the sheep took no notice of them.
9 I am the gate.
Anyone who enters through me will be safe: (C3)
he will go freely in and out·
and be sure of finding pasture. (C3)
10 The thief comes
only to steal and kill and destroy. (C2)
I have come
so that they may have life
and have it to the full.
11 I am the good shepherd:
the good shepherd is one who lays down his life for his sheep.
12 The hired man, since he is not the shepherd
and the sheep do not belong to him,
abandons the sheep and runs away
as soon as he sees a wolf coming, (C2)
and then the wolf attacks and scatters the sheep;
13 this is because he is only a hired man
and has no concern for the sheep. (C2)
14 I am the good shepherd;
I know my own
and my own know me,
15 just as the Father knows me
and I know the Father;

JOHN

and I lay down my life for my sheep.
16 And there are other sheep I have
that are not of this fold,
and these I have to lead as well.
They too will listen to my voice,
and there will be only one flock,
and one shepherd.
17 The Father loves me,
because I lay down my life
in order to take it up again.
18 No one takes it from me;
I lay it down of my own free will,
and as it is in my power to lay it down,
so it is in my power to take it up again;
and this is the command I have been given
by my Father."

19 These words caused disagreement among
20 the Jews. ·Many said, "He is possessed, he is raving; why bother to listen to him?"
21 Others said, "These are not the words of a man possessed by a devil: could a devil open the eyes of the blind?"

VI. THE FEAST OF DEDICATION

Jesus claims to be the Son of God

22 It was the time when the feast of Dedication was being celebrated in Jerusalem. It
23 was winter, ·and Jesus was in the Temple walking up and down in the Portico of Solo-
24 mon. ·The Jews gathered round him and said, "How much longer are you going to keep us in suspense? If you are the Christ, tell us
25 plainly." ·Jesus replied:

"I have told you, but you do not believe.
The works I do in my Father's name are my
    witness;
26 but you do not believe,
because you are no sheep of mine.

JOHN

27 The sheep that belong to me listen to my (c3)
   voice;
   I know them and they follow me.
28 I give them eternal life; (c3)
   they will never be lost
   and no one will ever steal them from me.
29 The Father who gave them to me is greater
      than anyone,
   and no one can steal from the Father.
30 The Father and I are one."

31 32 The Jews fetched stones to stone him, ·so (c2)
Jesus said to them, "I have done many good
works for you to see, works from my Father;
33 for which of these are you stoning me?" ·The
Jews answered him, "We are not stoning you
for doing a good work but for blasphemy: you
are only a man and you claim to be God." (c2)
34 Jesus answered:

"Is it not written in your Law:
I said, you are gods?[b]
35 So the Law uses the word gods
   of those to whom the word of God was addressed,
   and scripture cannot be rejected.
36 Yet you say to someone the Father has consecrated and sent into the world
   'You are blaspheming,' (c2)
   because he says 'I am the Son of God.'
37 If I am not doing my Father's work,
   there is no need to believe me;
38 but if I am doing it,
   then even if you refuse to believe in me, (c2)
   at least believe in the work I do; (c1)
   then you will know for sure
   that the Father is in me and I am in the Father."

39 They wanted to arrest him then, but he (c2)
eluded them.

b. Ps 82:6

Jesus withdraws to the other side of the Jordan

40 He went back again to the far side of the Jordan to stay in the district where John had 41 once been baptizing. ·Many people who came to him there said, "John gave no signs, 42 but all he said about this man was true"; ·and many of them believed in him.

(C1)

The resurrection of Lazarus

11 ¹There was a man named Lazarus who lived in the village of Bethany with the two sisters, Mary and Martha, and he was 2 ill.—·It was the same Mary, the sister of the sick man Lazarus, who anointed the Lord with ointment and wiped his feet with her 3 hair. ·The sisters sent this message to Jesus, 4 "Lord, the man you love is ill." ·On receiving the message, Jesus said, "This sickness will end not in death but in God's glory, and through it the Son of God will be glorified."

5 Jesus loved Martha and her sister and 6 Lazarus, ·yet when he heard that Lazarus was ill he stayed where he was for two more days 7 before saying to the disciples, "Let us go to 8 Judaea." ·The disciples said, "Rabbi, it is not long since the Jews wanted to stone you; are 9 you going back again?" ·Jesus replied:

(C2)

"Are there not twelve hours in the day?

A man can walk in the daytime without stumbling
because he has the light of this world to see by;
10 but if he walks at night he stumbles,
because there is no light to guide him."

11   He said that and then added, "Our friend Lazarus is resting, I am going to wake him."
12 The disciples said to him, "Lord, if he is able
13 to rest he is sure to get better." ·The phrase Jesus used referred to the death of Lazarus, but they thought that by "rest" he meant
14 "sleep," so ·Jesus put it plainly, "Lazarus is
15 dead; ·and for your sake I am glad I was not (C1) there because now you will believe. But let
16 us go to him." ·Then Thomas—known as the Twin—said to the other disciples, "Let us go (C3) too, and die with him."

17   On arriving, Jesus found that Lazarus had been in the tomb for four days already.
18 Bethany is only about two miles from Jerusa-
19 lem, ·and many Jews had come to Martha and Mary to sympathize with them over their
20 brother. ·When Martha heard that Jesus had (C3) come she went to meet him. Mary remained
21 sitting in the house. ·Martha said to Jesus, "If you had been here, my brother would not
22 have died, ·but I know that, even now, whatever you ask of God, he will grant you." (C1)
23 "Your brother," said Jesus to her, "will rise

where he comes from.' The man replied, 'Now here is an astonishing thing! He has opened my eyes, and you don't know where he comes from! We know that God doesn't listen to sinners, but God does listen to men who are devout and do his will. Ever since the world began it is unheard of for anyone to open the eyes of a man who was born blind; if this man were not from God, he couldn't do a thing.' 'Are you trying to teach us,' they replied, 'and you a sinner through and through, since you were born!' And they drove him away."(50)

3. Things have not changed much over the years, have they, Lord? Today, people - even intelligent, responsible people - still defy truth and logic to hold positions that they regard as advantageous to them. Abortion is a case in point. Anyone who has ever had even an elementary course in biology knows that once conception occurs an entirely new being comes into existence having the same nature as its parents. Thus a being biologically conceived by human parents is a human being from the moment of his or her conception. Yet to what great lengths many pro-abortionists will go to either deny this truth or say that there is no certainty that this is so.

4. When it comes to the doctrine that You are fully God, as well as fully man, how many there are who deny this truth also. Yet, at the same time they correctly maintain that Scripture is the revealed word of God.

Consequently, they go to great lengths trying to convince people that Scripture does not really mean what it clearly teaches about You.

5. This same sort of thing can be said, for example, about divorce and remarriage, and homosexuality and premarital relations. They might well argue, though falsely, that these practices are not sinful, but to claim that they are not really condemned by Your revealed word in Scripture makes no sense at all.

6. Next, Jesus, we read with pleasure the passage about You as the Good Shepherd and the Gate of the sheepfold.(51) Indeed, You alone are the Good Shepherd Who laid down Your life for Your sheep so that they might have life to the full. And You also are the Gate of the sheepfold, so that anyone who enters by You will be safe. And in plainer language, St. Peter said elsewhere that only in Your Name could we be saved.(52)

7. Thank You, Lord, for becoming man for us sinners, and for sacrificing Yourself for us on the altar of the Cross. May we always follow You, the Good Shepherd, Who loves Your sheep. May we always be Your true sheep who listen to Your voice so that we may have eternal life and never be lost.(53)

8. Jesus, at the end of Your discourse about the Good Shepherd, You said, "The Father and I are one."(54) Clearly, You meant that You too were divine. And there is no mistaking that the Jewish leaders thought

You were claiming this since, believing You were blaspheming, they took us stones to kill You, crying out, "You are only a man and you claim to be God."*(55)*

9. Yet in spite of this, as we have already noted, the belief that You are (were) only a man and that You never claimed to be otherwise is widely held in our day by those who regard themselves as Christians. Of course, if You were only a man, You would be a sinner like the rest of us and therefore incapable of taking away our sins. Nor should we adore You, since adoration is reserved only for God. *(See Ac 10:26 and "The Catholic Catechism," pp. 144-145.)*

10. Lord, may Your Holy Spirit always inspire us to confess Your divinity and worship You as true God.

11. Finally, Lord, we read in today's meditation about Your miraculous raising of Lazarus to life.*(56)* There seems to be no question that You performed this miracle as a sign pointing to Your own bodily Resurrection from the dead.*(57)* And it is in

the power of Your Resurrection that we too shall be raised up bodily from death at the end of time.*(58)* But You also performed the miracle as a sign pointing to Your messiahship.*(59)* Moreover, the resurrection of Lazarus indicated, as well, Your loving concern for him and his sisters, Martha and Mary.*(60)* Nor should we forget that this incident demonstrated, too, Your humanity, since St. John tells us You were in great distress and wept and sighed "straight from the heart."*(61)*

12. Few people today, Jesus, would deny that You are (were) human, whereas in the early centuries of Christianity there were those who did have trouble accepting Your humanity. This was because they reasoned that God could have nothing to do with material things such as the human body. Consequently, they concluded that You assumed only a phantom-like appearance of humanity. And in spite of what we have just said, there also exist in our own day those who tend to stress Your divinity to the neglect of Your humanity, thus often giving

the impression that You are only divine. Actually, we should always keep in mind that You are both divine and human.

13. You Who are God loved us so much that You became one of us, except for sin, and You really as man suffered and died for us on the Cross, and were raised from the dead, so that we could share in Your divinity for all eternity in our bodies together with our spiritual souls.

14. Please, Lord, grant us to be constant in confidence and seed-charity so that with pure consciences we can die in Your peace and obtain the reward of eternal life. Amen.

Try to read these Scripture passages and meditations in a reflective manner every day. The Holy Spirit will reveal more insights to you each time you do so.

Please read and meditate on Chapter II, Paragraphs 32 to 38 of Peaceful Seed Living, Volume I.

WEEK 2 DAY 1
The Gospel of St. John
Chapter 12:1-34

The anointing at Bethany

1 12 Six days before the Passover, Jesus went to Bethany, where Lazarus was,
2 whom he had raised from the dead. ·They gave a dinner for him there; Martha waited on them and Lazarus was among those at
3 table. ·Mary brought in a pound of very costly ointment, pure nard, and with it (C3)

JOHN

anointed the feet of Jesus, wiping them with her hair; the house was full of the scent of
4 the ointment. ·Then Judas Iscariot—one of his disciples, the man who was to betray
5 him—said, ·"Why wasn't this ointment sold for three hundred denarii, and the money
6 given to the poor?" ·He said this, not because he cared about the poor, but because he was a thief; he was in charge of the common fund and used to help himself to the contributions.
7 So Jesus said, "Leave her alone; she had to
8 keep this scent for the day of my burial. ·You have the poor with you always, you will not always have me."

9 Meanwhile a large number of Jews heard that he was there and came not only on account of Jesus but also to see Lazarus whom
10 he had raised from the dead. ·Then the chief
11 priests decided to kill Lazarus as well, ·since it was on his account that many of the Jews were leaving them and believing in Jesus.

The Messiah enters Jerusalem

12 The next day the crowds who had come up for the festival heard that Jesus was on his
13 way to Jerusalem. ·They took branches of palm and went out to meet him, shouting, *"Hosanna! Blessings on the King of Israel,*
14 *who comes in the name of the Lord."*[a] ·Jesus found a young donkey and mounted it—as
15 scripture says: ·*Do not be afraid, daughter of Zion; see, your king is coming, mounted on*
16 *the colt of a donkey.*[b] ·At the time his disciples did not understand this, but later, after Jesus had been glorified, they remembered that this had been written about him and that this was in fact how they had received him.
17 All who had been with him when he called Lazarus out of the tomb and raised him from the dead were telling how they had witnessed
18 it; ·it was because of this, too, that the crowd

came out to meet him: they had heard that
19 he had given this sign. ·Then the Pharisees
said to one another, "You see, there is noth- (C3)
ing you can do; look, the whole world is running after him!"

Jesus foretells his death and subsequent glorification

20   Among those who went up to worship at
21 the festival were some Greeks.*c* ·These ap-
proached Philip, who came from Bethsaida
in Galilee, and put this request to him, "Sir,
22 we should like to see Jesus." ·Philip went to
tell Andrew, and Andrew and Philip together
went to tell Jesus.
23   Jesus replied to them:

"Now the hour has come
for the Son of Man to be glorified.
24 I tell you, most solemnly,
unless a wheat grain falls on the ground and
    dies,
it remains only a single grain;
but if it dies,
it yields a rich harvest. (C3)
25 Anyone who loves his life loses it; (C2)
anyone who hates his life in this world
will keep it for the eternal life. (C3)
26 If a man serves me, he must follow me, (C3)
wherever I am, my servant will be there too.
If anyone serves me, my Father will honor (C3)
   him.

27 Now my soul is troubled.
What shall I say:
Father, save me from this hour?
But it was for this very reason that I have come to this hour.
28 Father, glorify your name!"

A voice came from heaven, "I have glorified it, and I will glorify it again."
29 People standing by, who heard this, said it was a clap of thunder; others said, "It was
30 an angel speaking to him." ·Jesus answered, "It was not for my sake that this voice came, but for yours.
31 "Now sentence is being passed on this world;
now the prince of this world is to be overthrown.*d*
32 And when I am lifted up from the earth,
I shall draw all men to myself."

33 By these words he indicated the kind of
34 death he would die. ·The crowd answered, "The Law has taught us that the Christ will remain for ever. How can you say, 'The Son of Man must be lifted up?' Who is this Son of Man?"

Week 2 Day 1
Four C's Meditations
on St. John 12:1-34

1. Jesus, Divine Savior, in today's reading, St. John began to describe the last few days of Your life which led to Your Crucifixion. We were told that Your final agony was only six days away. And in yesterday's reading we learned that the Jewish chief priests and the Pharisees had issued orders to have You arrested.

2. The opening scene in today's reading takes place in Bethany where Lazarus and his sisters, Martha and Mary, lived.*(62)* You had gone to dinner with these three, and with some of Your disciples, to the home of a certain Simon the Leper. While You were there, John tells us that Mary anointed Your feet (which perhaps were fatigued from walking) with a very expensive ointment. Moreover, we are told that she wiped Your feet with her own hair. Undoubtedly, Mary could have anointed You with a less costly ointment, such as lanolin or olive oil. And she certainly could have used a towel to wipe Your feet instead of using her own hair. But Mary loved You in a manner that was selfless. She pulled out all the stops, so to speak. No expense was too great, as far as she was concerned, when it came to serving You, Lord. This would especially seem to be the case, if she realized that Your death was near and wanted to do this as an expression of her gratitude for Your selfless love for her.

3. (Early tradition identifies this Mary with Mary Magdalene who had previously lived a life of a woman of ill-repute, but eventually she became one of Jesus' loyal followers, having received from Him the forgiveness of her sins.)

4. Jesus, when Judas objected to the "waste" of the expensive ointment, it was like saying that an artist wastes his time in spending years to train himself in his craft, or that he wastes his time spending months or even years in painting a mural or a fresco, when he could have been painting cars, or drawing cartoons by the hundreds of dozens during the same time span.

5. Despite his statement to the contrary, Judas, of course, was not really interested in the poor, whereas You were, Lord. Your concern was clearly indicated when You counseled the rich young ruler to give his wealth to the poor *(63)* and when You said that You were sent to preach the Gospel to the poor.*(64)*

6. Even if Judas had been serious about helping the needy, You rightly pointed out, Lord, that they will always be present to be helped, but that You were soon to die. Therefore, Mary felt urged to do something quickly that would reflect her love for You. And surely, as Your disciple, she had become the type of person who was also concerned with the plight of the poor.

7. Next, Lord Jesus, we meditated on Your

instruction on seed-charity. Here You announced that You were soon about to sacrifice Your life in order to draw all men to Yourself. Your following words perfectly describe the *"Peaceful Seed Living"* spirituality of The Apostolate for Family Consecration.

8. "Now the hour has come for the Son of Man to be glorified. I tell you most solemnly, unless a wheat grain falls on the ground and dies, it remains only a single grain; but if it dies, it yields a rich harvest. Anyone who loves his life loses it; anyone who hates his life in this world will keep it for the eternal life. If a man serves me, he must follow me.... Now my soul is troubled. What shall I say: Father save me from this hour? But it was for this very reason that I have come to this hour.... And when I am lifted up from the earth, I shall draw all men to myself."(65)

9. Jesus, if each of us would truly imitate You by dying to self, that is, to our self-will, all of the world's ills would disappear. There would be no more fighting and bitterness in families. There would be no more crime, no

more violence, no more war, no more grinding poverty. There would instead be paradise on earth; love, happiness, peace, and purity of heart would reign.

10. Truly Lord, Your Kingdom will come when Your Father's will is done on earth as it is in Heaven. Your Kingdom will come when there is enough reparation made through prayer, good works and fervent reception of the sacraments to offset the divisive effects of sin that separate us from the Holy Trinity.

11. As You said, Lord, a seed must fall on the ground to die before it can be transformed into a plant yielding a rich harvest. But there is a fundamental difference between a plant's seed and ourselves. A seed has no free will. It simply does what You have programmed it to do through its genetic structure. It cannot freely resist or fight back. We, on the other hand, not only have free will, but, because of our fallen nature, we almost instinctively resist dying to our selfishness. Thus, too often, it is easier for us to be selfish than to be charitable beings, glorifying You and serving the material and spiritual needs of

others. *(For information on our Fall, see "The Catholic Catechism," pp. 119-120.)*

12. Jesus, it is only through the use of Your grace, earned for us on the Cross, that we have the strength to overcome our tendency to self-centeredness. Moreover, it is Your example of complete and constant selflessness, and the examples of Your saints, that help motivate us to use this grace. And as we use it, we not only die to self-centeredness, we also share in Your own divine nature giving us access to eternal life.*(66)*

13. But even with Your example and Your grace, it still hurts, at times, for us to follow in Your footsteps. Here sincere and fervent prayer is of great help, because through it You respond by inspiring us to take up our own crosses and follow You.*(67)*

14. One last thought, Lord. Most worthwhile goals in life are not obtained without some degree of self-sacrifice. Therefore, it shouldn't be surprising that the most worthwhile goal of all, eternal life with God, demands a total self-surrender to You and Your will for us. Please, Jesus, always encourage us to die to self and to live for You, and for others for Your sake. Amen.

Try to read these Scripture passages and meditations in a reflective manner every day. The Holy Spirit will reveal more insights to you each time you do so.

Please read and meditate on Chapter III, Paragraphs 1 to 7 of Peaceful Seed Living, Volume I.

WEEK 2 DAY 2
The Gospel of St. John
Chapters 12:35-13:20

35 ·Jesus then said:

"The light will be with you only a little longer
  now.
Walk while you have the light,
or the dark will overtake you;
he who walks in the dark does not know
  where he is going.
36 While you still have the light,
believe in the light   (C1)
and you will become sons of light."   (C3)

Having said this, Jesus left them and kept himself hidden.

Conclusion: the unbelief of the Jews

37 Though they had been present when he gave so many signs, they did not believe (C2)
38 in him; ·this was to fulfill the words of the prophet Isaiah: *Lord, who could believe what we have heard said, and to whom has the power of the Lord been revealed?*[e]
39 Indeed, they were unable to believe because,

JOHN

40 as Isaiah says again: ·*He has blinded their* (c2) *eyes, he has hardened their heart, for fear they should see with their eyes and understand with their heart, and turn to me for healing.*ƒ

41 Isaiah said this when he saw his glory,*g* and his words referred to Jesus.

42 And yet there were many who did believe (c1) in him, even among the leading men, but they did not admit it, through fear of the Pharisees and fear of being expelled from the syna-

43 gogue: ·they put honor from men before the (c2) honor that comes from God.

44 Jesus declared publicly:
"Whoever believes in me (c1)
believes not in me
but in the one who sent me, (c1)
45 and whoever sees me,
sees the one who sent me.
46 I, the light, have come into the world,
so that whoever believes in me (c1)
need not stay in the dark any more.
47 If anyone hears my words and does not keep (c2) them faithfully,
it is not I who shall condemn him,
since I have come not to condemn the world,
but to save the world:
48 he who rejects me and refuses my words (c2)
has his judge already:
the word itself that I have spoken
will be his judge on the last day.
49 For what I have spoken does not come from myself;
no, what I was to say, what I had to speak,
was commanded by the Father who sent me,
50 and I know that his commands mean eternal life.
And therefore what the Father has told me
is what I speak."

JOHN

B. THE LAST SUPPER

Jesus washes his disciples' feet

13 ¹ It was before the festival of the Passover, and Jesus knew that the hour had come for him to pass from this world to the Father. He had always loved those who were his in the world, but now he showed how perfect his love was. ² They were at supper, and the devil had already put it into the mind of Judas Iscariot son of Simon, to betray him. ·Jesus knew that the Father had put everything into his hands, and that he had come from God and was ⁴ returning to God, ·and he got up from table, removed his outer garment and, taking a ⁵ towel, wrapped it round his waist; ·he then poured water into a basin and began to wash the disciples' feet*a* and to wipe them with the towel he was wearing.

⁶ He came to Simon Peter, who said to him, "Lord, are you going to wash my feet?" ⁷ Jesus answered, "At the moment you do not know what I am doing, but later you will ⁸ understand." ·"Never!" said Peter. "You shall never wash my feet." Jesus replied, "If I do not wash you, you can have nothing in ⁹ common with me." ·"Then, Lord," said Simon Peter, "not only my feet, but my hands ¹⁰ and my head as well!" ·Jesus said, "No one who has taken a bath needs washing, he is clean all over. You too are clean, though not ¹¹ all of you are." ·He knew who was going to betray him, that was why he said, "though not all of you are."

¹² When he had washed their feet and put on his clothes again he went back to the table. "Do you understand" he said "what I have ¹³ done to you? ·You call me Master and Lord, ¹⁴ and rightly; so I am. ·If I, then, the Lord and

Master, have washed your feet, you should
15 wash each other's feet. •I have given you an (c3)
example so that you may copy what I have
done to you.

16 "I tell you most solemnly,
no servant is greater than his master,
no messenger is greater than the man who
sent him.
17 "Now that you know this, happiness will (c3)
18 be yours if you behave accordingly. •I am not
speaking about all of you: I know the ones
I have chosen; but what scripture says must
be fulfilled: *Someone who shares my table* (c2)
rebels against me.[b]

19 "I tell you this now, before it happens,
so that when it does happen
you may believe that I am He. (c1)
20 I tell you most solemnly,
whoever welcomes the one I send welcomes (c3)
me,
and whoever welcomes me welcomes the (c3)
one who sent me."

114

**Week 2 Day 2
Four C's Meditations
on St. John 12:35-13:20**

1. *Most Sacred Heart of Jesus, in today's reading, You told the crowds in Jerusalem to believe in the Light so that they could become the sons of Light.(68)* You and Your teaching, of course, are the Light which illuminates the truths we must accept and the paths we must follow if we are to obtain inner peace and lasting happiness.

2. Thankfully, we have Scripture which reveals to us this Light. And as we meditate on Scripture, with a pure heart and with the assistance of God the Holy Spirit, we can see the Light of Your truth more and more clearly, and be motivated to believe and act upon it more fervently. *(Sacred Tradition is also a source of revealed truths. For information about this see "The Catholic Catechism," pp. 46-48.)*

3. Unfortunately, this Light is not always clearly seen. Personal sin can obscure it, but

so can misunderstanding of its true meaning.*(69)*

4. Please, Lord, help us to discover the light of Your truth, and when we have found it, help us to believe and practice it, thus avoiding the darkness that leads to spiritual death.

5. Jesus, You also told the crowds in Jerusalem, that "The light will be with you only a little longer now. Walk while you have the light or the dark will overtake you...."*(70)* You had reference to the fact that You would soon be leaving this world and You wanted the crowds to receive Your doctrine of salvation before You left. On the other hand, Your statement also has meaning for us today. That is, we are in this world for only a short time, relatively speaking, and we don't know when we will depart from it. Consequently, the sooner we turn to You and receive the light of Your teaching and apply it to our lives, the better. Certainly, if we were to deliberately put off accepting You as Savior, and death caught us unprepared, we would quite likely find ourselves in eternal darkness "where there will be weeping and grinding of teeth."*(71)*

6. Lord, we never know when it will be too late to repent of our sins and receive You as the Light of our souls. May we constantly believe and trust in You, keep ourselves free from sin, and sow seeds of self-sacrifice for You and for others. Thus when death comes we will be ready to be taken into Your arms

and receive the rewards of eternal peace, joy and happiness.

7. Jesus, in today's reading, St. John wrote that there were men in Jerusalem who believed in You but were afraid to admit it openly, because they were afraid that the Pharisees would expel them from the synagogues. St. John noted that they were more concerned with the honor of men than with God.*(72)*

8. I am afraid, Lord, that many of us today act in a similar fashion. A glaring example would be those in positions of prestige and influence who say that they personally subscribe to Your doctrine about the sanctity of human life, yet in practice they side with powerful interests which deny this truth and promote the destruction of innocent babies in their mothers' wombs. Can there be anything worse than the destruction of the innocent?

9. Then there are those who regard personal friendships more highly than giving honor to You. Consequently, they refuse to discuss religious convictions with many of their friends for fear of offending them. You, however, warned against such cowardice. In the Parable of the Talents, for instance, You taught that the man who was afraid to use what God had given him was severely punished.*(73)* You also taught, Lord, that those who are ashamed of You and Your teaching, You will be ashamed of in Heaven.*(74)*

10. Please help us not only to believe in

You, but also to love You above all else, along with the Father and the Holy Spirit. Then we will be able to love ourselves, and our neighbors as ourselves. - All honor and glory be given to You Blessed One in Three.

11. Finally, Jesus, we read St. John's account of Your washing the disciples' feet on the occasion of the Last Supper.(75) By this loving and humble act You have shown us, in a way that mere words could not, what it means to be a Christian in a position of authority. Such a person is to love and humbly serve those who are placed in his charge.

12. Obviously, St. Peter was not used to being served by superiors, as his words well indicate. And it can be reasonably assumed that in his day as in our own, many, if not most, who are in positions of authority take advantage of their positions to serve themselves at the expense of those whom they should be serving.

13. Your act of washing the disciples' feet, however, Lord, leaves no doubt as to what a person in authority is expected to do. He is to use his position to serve those "under" him. He is to do what is in their best interest.

14. Serving those over whom a person has authority does not mean, of course, a relinquishing of authority. Parents, for example, should clearly be in charge of their children. Employers should be in charge of their employees, and pastors in charge of their parishioners' spiritual welfare.

15. Nonetheless, a person in authority has the awesome responsibility of really being the servant of his charges through the exercise of seed-charity. And all who are in positions of authority will have to render You an accounting, Our Savior, on the Day of Judgment.

16. Lord Jesus, You came to earth to serve and not to be served.(76) Please help those in positions of authority to realize that they are to do likewise. Thus, they will obtain the happiness You promised. Amen.

The more you re-read these Scriptures and meditations, the more you will get out of them.

Please read and meditate on Chapter III, Paragraphs 8 to 23 of Peaceful Seed Living, Volume I.

WEEK 2 DAY 3
The Gospel of St. John
Chapters 13:21-14:1

The treachery of Judas foretold

21 Having said this, Jesus was troubled in spirit and declared, "I tell you most solemnly, one of you will betray me." •The dis- (C2)
22 ciples looked at one another, wondering
23 which he meant. •The disciple Jesus loved
24 was reclining next to Jesus; •Simon Peter signed to him and said, "Ask who it is he
25 means," •so leaning back on Jesus' breast he
26 said, "Who is it, Lord?" •"It is the one," replied Jesus, "to whom I give the piece of bread that I shall dip in the dish." He dipped the piece of bread and gave it to Judas son
27 of Simon Iscariot. •At that instant, after Judas had taken the bread, Satan entered him. Jesus (C2) then said, "What you are going to do, do
28 quickly." •None of the others at table under-
29 stood the reason he said this. •Since Judas had charge of the common fund, some of them thought Jesus was telling him, "Buy what we need for the festival," or telling him
30 to give something to the poor. •As soon as (C2)

JOHN

Judas had taken the piece of bread he went out. Night had fallen.

31 When he had gone Jesus said:

"Now has the Son of Man been glorified,
and in him God has been glorified.
32 If God has been glorified in him,
God will in turn glorify him in himself,*c*
and will glorify him very soon.

Farewell discourses

33 "My little children,
I shall not be with you much longer.

You will look for me, (C3)
and, as I told the Jews,
where I am going,
you cannot come.
34 I give you a new commandment:
love one another;
just as I have loved you, (C3)
you also must love one another. (C3)
35 By this love you have for one another,
everyone will know that you are my disci- (C3)
ples."

36 Simon Peter said, "Lord, where are you going?" Jesus replied, "Where I am going you cannot follow me now; you will follow 37 me later." ·Peter said to him, "Why can't I follow you now? I will lay down my life for (C3) 38 you." ·"Lay down your life for me?" answered Jesus. "I tell you most solemnly, before the cock crows you will have disowned me three times. (C2)

14 1 "Do not let your hearts be troubled. Trust in God still, and trust in me. (C1)

121

**Week 2 Day 3
Four C's Meditations
on St. John 13:21-14:1**

1.   Jesus, today, we read of Judas Iscariot who would soon betray You.*(77)* Although we would rather not think about it, the thought does not leave our minds that we, too, are capable of betraying You. We can betray You, for instance, when we fail to sacrifice ourselves for others, since You clearly taught that helping those in need is the same as helping You. Thus, Lord, we should love You in everyone who comes into our lives.

2.   "'Go away from me, with your curse upon you, to the eternal fire prepared for the devil and his angels. For I was hungry and you never gave me food; I was thirsty and you never gave me drink; I was a stranger and you never made me welcome, naked and you never clothed me, sick and in prison and you never visited me.... I tell you solemnly, insofar

as you neglected to do this to one of the least of these, you neglected to do it to me.' And they will go away to eternal punishment, and the virtuous to eternal life."(78)

3. On the spiritual plane, Lord, You have chosen us Christians to be Your representatives in the world so that others may be converted to You. Therefore, when we fail to represent You to others, we betray You, since we have neglected to be Your channels of saving grace. And of course we betray others also since they are denied, at least by us, the opportunity of receiving You and salvation.

4. When we commit mortal sin we betray You as well, since, in being cut off from Your friendship, our effectiveness in reaching others for Your sake is greatly diminished, if not destroyed altogether.

5. Jesus, Lord, we pray that we never betray You. May our hearts always be pure in this regard. And may our love for You, and for others for Your sake, always be strengthened by Your grace, so that thoughts

of betrayal may quickly vanish.

6. Next, Lord, we meditated on Your New Commandment which states that we are to love one another *as You have loved us.*(79) You, then, are the standard. You are the measure Whom we are to imitate in our love of neighbor. This commandment is a much more exacting law than its Old Testament counterpart where we are taught simply to love our neighbors as ourselves.

7. How have You loved us, Lord? Literally to death. Yes, Your love for us is the supreme example of self-sacrifice. What is especially amazing is that You loved us while we were still sinners, offering up Your life for us on the Cross.(80)

8. Lord, only to the degree that we sacrifice ourselves for others, as You did for us, can we find genuine happiness. Yet there is a widespread notion today that real happiness, often called self-fulfillment, comes from being "self-assertive," "aggressive," and from "doing what we want." In essence this is nothing more than a prescription for selfishness which, if generally followed, can only lead to the break-up of society. Whereas, a life of self-sacrificing seed-charity, if practiced on a wide scale, will lead to a peaceful, harmonious society.

9. It is important for us to keep in mind, Lord, that there is no way we can constantly love one another as You have loved us, unless we first love You, the Father and the

Holy Spirit. As we love You with all of our heart, mind, soul and strength, You give us the grace of seed-charity to love others as You have loved us. Lord, may we always love You above everything else and love others as You have loved us.

10. Jesus, in the very first verse of chapter fourteen, You give our anxiety-prone age a relevant precept. "Do not let your hearts be troubled. Trust in God still and trust in me."*(81)* In other words, "Do not worry. You can stop being anxiety-ridden by trusting in God the Father and by trusting in Me." In these insecure times, Lord, help us to truly look to You as Our Source and not to the temporary world.

11. How often we are told by our friends, "Don't worry." But how seldom we are reminded, Lord, that the only real remedy for chronic worry is to have confidence in You. As we trust in You, Lord, all our needs and problems will be handled by Your providential action, as You have promised.

12. "Can any of you, for all his worrying, add one single cubit to the span of life?.... So do not worry; do not say, 'What are we to eat? What are we to drink? How are we to be clothed? It is the pagans who set their hearts on all these things. Your heavenly Father knows you need them all. Set your hearts on his kingdom first, and on his righteousness, and all these things will be given to you as well. So do not worry about tomorrow: tomorrow will take care of itself. Each day has enough trouble of its own."*(82)*

13. Thus, if we put our confidence in God's loving providence, all of our real needs will be taken care of.

14. Lord, how often we have become paralyzed by needless and fruitless anxiety. It is needless because You will meet all of our needs and concerns, if we turn to You with a trusting heart. It is fruitless because anxiety turns us in on ourselves and saps our strength to act constructively and rationally. Please strengthen our confidence in You, Lord, day by day. Amen.

Please read and meditate on Chapter III, Paragraphs 24 to 34 of Peaceful Seed Living, Volume I.

Also re-read and meditate on today's Scriptures.

WEEK 2 DAY 4
The Gospel of St. John
Chapter 14:2-31

2 There are many rooms in my Father's house;
if there were not, I should have told you.
I am going now to prepare a place for you,
3 and after I have gone and prepared you a place,
I shall return to take you with me;
so that where I am
you may be too.
4 You know the way to the place where I am going."

5 Thomas said, "Lord, we do not know where you are going, so how can we know 6 the way?" ·Jesus said:

"I am the Way, the Truth and the Life.
No one can come to the Father except through me.
7 If you know me, you know my Father too.
From this moment you know him and have seen him."

8 Philip said, "Lord, let us see the Father
9 and then we shall be satisfied." ·"Have I been with you all this time, Philip," said Jesus to him, "and you still do not know me?

> "To have seen me is to have seen the Father,
> so how can you say, 'Let us see the Father'?
> 10 Do you not believe (c1)
> that I am in the Father and the Father is in me?
> The words I say to you I do not speak as from myself:
> it is the Father, living in me, who is doing this work.
> 11 You must believe me when I say (c1)
> that I am in the Father and the Father is in me;
> believe it on the evidence of this work, (c1)
> if for no other reason.
> 12 I tell you most solemnly, (c1)
> whoever believes in me (c3)
> will perform the same works as I do myself,
> he will perform even greater works, (c3)
> because I am going to the Father.
> 13 Whatever you ask for in my name I will do, (c1)
> so that the Father may be glorified in the Son. (c3)
> 14 If you ask for anything in my name, (c1)
> I will do it. (c3)
> 15 If you love me you will keep my commandments. (c3)
> 16 I shall ask the Father,
> and he will give you another Advocate[a]
> to be with you for ever,
> 17 that Spirit of truth
> whom the world can never receive
> since it neither sees nor knows him;
> but you know him,

JOHN

because he is with you, he is in you.
18 I will not leave you orphans;
I will come back to you.
19 In a short time the world will no longer see me;
but you will see me,
because I live and you will live.
20 On that day
you will understand that I am in my Father
and you in me and I in you.
21 Anybody who receives my commandments and keeps them (C1)
will be one who loves me;
and anybody who loves me will be loved by my Father, (C3) (C3)
and I shall love him and show myself to him."

22 Judas[b]—this was not Judas Iscariot—said to him, "Lord, what is all this about? Do you intend to show yourself to us and not to the 23 world?" ·Jesus replied:

"If anyone loves me he will keep my word, (C3)
and my Father will love him,
and we shall come to him
and make our home with him.
24 Those who do not love me do not keep my words. (C2)
And my word is not my own:
it is the word of the one who sent me.
25 I have said these things to you
while still with you;
26 but the Advocate, the Holy Spirit,
whom the Father will send in my name,
will teach you everything
and remind you of all I have said to you.

b. "Judas, brother of James" in Lk 6:16 and Ac 1:13; the Thaddaeus of Mt 10:3 and Mk 3:18.

27 Peace[c] I bequeath to you,
my own peace I give you,
a peace the world cannot give, this is my gift to you.
Do not let your hearts be troubled or afraid.

28 You heard me say: (C2)
I am going away, and shall return.
If you loved me you would have been glad to know that I am going to the Father, (C3)
for the Father is greater than I.

29 I have told you this now before it happens,
so that when it does happen you may believe. (C1)

30 I shall not talk with you any longer,
because the prince of this world is on his way. (C2)
He has no power over me,

31 but the world must be brought to know that I love the Father
and that I am doing exactly what the Father told me.
Come now, let us go.

**Week 2 Day 4
Four C's Meditations
on St. John 14:2-31**

1. Most Merciful Savior, You are truly the Way, the Truth and the Life. *(83)* You are the only Way to true and unending happiness, joy and peace with our heavenly Father. You alone are the fullness of Truth that saves us from error and points us to the way of salvation. And You are the perfect Life Who gives supernatural existence to our souls and allows us to share in Your divine nature, both now and in Heaven.

2. Lord, constantly grant us faith, trust, pure consciences, and seed-charity which we need to remain in You Who are the Way, the Truth and the Life. And, for being these things, may we always praise and thank You.

3. Most Sacred Heart of Jesus, You also said that if we believed in You we would not only perform the same works You did while

on earth, but that we would perform even greater works because You were going to the Father in Heaven.*(84)*

4. You obviously did not mean that through our faith in You we would perform greater works in a qualitative sense. Rather You meant that we Christians, working together, would perform greater works in a numerical sense only. And this is possible because when You returned to the Father You asked Him to send us the power of the Holy Spirit.*(85)*

5. Lord, through our faith in You, may we perform the works You desire so that others will be attracted to You, our only Savior.

6. Jesus, You also said in today's meditation that whatever we ask the Father for in Your Name will be granted.*(86)* In other words, You meant that whatever we ask for as Your representatives, and in accordance to Your will, will be granted,

7. Lord, You next said that if we love You, we would keep Your commandments.*(87)* This is certainly true. How could we really love You if we refused to keep Your commandments? Unfortunately, there are some who profess to love You, yet deliberately break Your precepts. This is like a husband who claims he really loves his wife, yet regularly beats her and has affairs with other women. He might have some sort of love for her, but it certainly is not the sacrificial seed-charity that is essential for a good marriage.

8. It only makes sense, Jesus, that if we

really loved You we would try very hard to please You by observing Your precepts. Help us, Lord, to keep them. And when we fail, grant us the gift of repentance so we can be reconciled with You and receive additional grace both to love You and do as You have commanded.

9. Jesus, You have promised us that the person who really loves You will be loved by You and the Father as well. And not only that, but both You and the Father will come and dwell in him together with the Holy Spirit.*(88)* In the light of this great mystery, we should recall frequently that our bodies are meant to be temples of the most Holy Trinity.*(89)* And when we love the Trinity with our lips, and with our thoughts and with our deeds, the Father, the Son and the Holy Spirit dwell within us offering us love and friendship.

10. Lord, whenever we think of Your divine presence within us, we are encouraged to remain in Your friendship and avoid sin. Therefore, may we recall Your indwelling presence often and be continually inspired to keep You, the Father and the Holy Spirit as our guests. And may we never drive You from us by polluting our bodies with that which displeases You.

11. Next, Our Savior, our attention was drawn to Your famous statement in which You said, "Peace I bequeath to you, my own peace I give you, a peace which the world cannot give, this is my gift to you."*(90)*

12. How the world longs for peace,

especially for peace in the soul. But this comes only from being in Your friendship, a friendship free of the contamination of sin and based on confidence (faith and hope) and seed-charity. This is truly the peace that comes from You, Most Merciful Lord, and not from the world.

13. Lord, this is also the peace that The Apostolate has in mind when it speaks of Peaceful Seed-Living. It is a peace that comes from applying Scripture's Four C's of confidence, conscience, seed-charity and constancy to one's life. Through Your Holy Spirit, Jesus, You inspired the authors of Sacred Scripture to write about the Four C's Formula for Peaceful Seed Living. Now may the same Spirit inspire us to apply them to our own lives so that we may always enjoy Your fruit of peace which surpasses all understanding and which the world cannot give. Amen.

Experience this gift of peace by slowly re-reading and meditating on the Scripture for today. Ask the Holy Spirit for this gift of peace.

Please read and meditate on Chapter III, Paragraphs 35 to 43 of Peaceful Seed Living, Volume I.

WEEK 2 DAY 5
The Gospel of St. John
Chapters 15:1-16:33

The true vine

1 **15** "I am the true vine,
and my Father is the vinedresser.
2 Every branch in me that bears no fruit (C2)
he cuts away,
and every branch that does bear fruit
he prunes
to make it bear even more.
3 You are pruned already, (C3)
by means of the word that I have spoken to you.
4 Make your home in me, as I make mine (C3)
in you.
As a branch cannot bear fruit all by
itself,
but must remain part of the vine, (C3)
neither can you unless you remain in (C4)
me.
5 I am the vine,
you are the branches.
Whoever remains in me, with me in (C4)
him,
bears fruit in plenty; (C3)
for cut off from me you can do nothing. (C2)

JOHN

6	Anyone who does not remain in me	(C2)
	is like a branch that has been thrown away	
	—he withers;	
	these branches are collected and thrown on the fire,	
	and they are burned.	(C3)
7	If you remain in me	(C4)
	and my words remain in you,	(C1)
	you may ask what you will	
	and you shall get it.	
8	It is to the glory of my Father that you should bear much fruit,	(C3)
	and then you will be my disciples.	
9	As the Father has loved me,	
	so I have loved you.	
	Remain in my love.	(C3)
10	If you keep my commandments	(C4)
	you will remain in my love,	(C3)
	just as I have kept my Father's commandments	(C4)
	and remain in his love.	
11	I have told you this	
	so that my own joy may be in you	
	and your joy be complete.	
12	This is my commandment:	
	love one another,	(C3)
	as I have loved you.	
13	A man can have no greater love	
	than to lay down his life for his friends.	(C3)
14	You are my friends,	
	if you do what I command you.	(C3)
15	I shall not call you servants any more,	
	because a servant does not know his master's business;	
	I call you friends,	
	because I have made known to you everything I have learned from my Father.	
16	You did not choose me,	
	no, I chose you;	
	and I commissioned you	

JOHN

    to go out and to bear fruit, (C3)
    fruit that will last; (C4)
    and then the Father will give you
    anything you ask him in my name. (C3)
17   What I command you
    is to love one another. (C3)

The hostile world

18   "If the world hates you, (C2)
    remember that it hated me before you. (C2)
19   If you belonged to the world,
    the world would love you as its own;
    but because you do not belong to the world, (C3)
    because my choice withdrew you from the world,
    therefore, the world hates you. (C2)
20   Remember the words I said to you:
    A servant is not greater than his master.
    If they persecuted me, (C2)
    they will persecute you too; (C2)
    if they kept my word,
    they will keep yours as well.
21   But it will be on my account that they will do all this,
    because they do not know the one who sent me.
22   If I had not come,
    if I had not spoken to them,
    they would have been blameless;
    but as it is they have no excuse for their sin. (C2)
23   Anyone who hates me hates my Father. (C2)
24   If I had not performed such works among them
    as no one else has ever done,
    they would be blameless;
    but as it is, they have seen all this,
    and still they hate both me and my Father. (C2)

25 But all this was only to fulfill the words written in their law:
*They hated me for no reason.*ᵃ (C2)
26 When the Advocate comes,
whom I shall send to you from the Father,
the Spirit of truth who issues from the Father,
he will be my witness.
27 And you too will be witnesses, (C1)
because you have been with me from (C3)
the outset.

16

1 "I have told you all this (C1)
so that your faith may not be shaken.
2 They will expel you from the synagogues, (C4)
and indeed the hour is coming (C2)
when anyone who kills you will think (C2)
he is doing a holy duty for God.
3 They will do these things (C2)
because they have never known either the Father or myself.
4 But I have told you all this,
so that when the time for it comes
you may remember that I told you.

The coming of the Advocate

"I did not tell you this from the outset,
because I was with you;
5 but now I am going to the one who sent me.

Not one of you has asked, 'Where are you going?'
6 Yet you are sad at heart because I have told you this. (C3)
7 Still, I must tell you the truth:
it is for your own good that I am going
because unless I go,
the Advocate will not come to you;
but if I do go,
I will send him to you.
8 And when he comes,
he will show the world how wrong it was,
about sin, (C2)
and about who was in the right,
and about judgment:
9 about sin: (C2)
proved by their refusal to believe in me; (C2)
10 about who was in the right:
proved by my going to the Father
and your seeing me no more;
11 about judgment:
proved by the prince of this world being already condemned.
12 I still have many things to say to you
but they would be too much for you now.
13 But when the Spirit of truth comes
he will lead you to the complete truth,
since he will not be speaking as from himself

JOHN

> but will say only what he has learned;
> and he will tell you of the things to come.

14 > He will glorify me,
> since all he tells you
> will be taken from what is mine.

15 > Everthing the Father has is mine;
> that is why I said:
> All he tells you
> will be taken from what is mine.

Jesus to return very soon

16 > "In a short time you will no longer see and then a short time later you will see me again."

17 Then some of his disciples said to one another, "What does he mean, 'In a short time you will no longer see me, and then a short time later you will see me again' and, 'I am
18 going to the Father'? ·What is this 'short time'? We don't know what he means."
19 Jesus knew that they wanted to question him, so he said, "You are asking one another what I meant by saying: In a short time you will no longer see me, and then a short time later you will see me again.

20 > "I tell you most solemnly,
> you will be weeping and wailing (c3)
> while the world will rejoice;
> you will be sorrowful, (c3)
> but your sorrow will turn to joy.

21 > A woman in childbirth suffers, (c3)
> because her time has come;
> but when she has given birth to the child she forgets the suffering
> in her joy that a man has been born into the world.

22 > So it is with you: you are sad now, (c3)
> but I shall see you again, and your (c3)

JOHN

      hearts will be full of joy,
and that joy no one shall take from (C4)
you.
23 When that day comes,
you will not ask me any questions.
I tell you most solemnly,
anything you ask for from the Fa- (C1)
ther
he will grant in my name. (C3)
24 Until now you have not asked for anything in my name.
Ask and you will receive, (C1)
and so your joy will be complete. (C3)
25 I have been telling you all this in metaphors,
the hour is coming
when I shall no longer speak to you in metaphors;
but tell you about the Father in plain words.
26 When that day comes (C1)
you will ask in my name;
and I do not say that I shall pray to the Father for you,
27 because the Father himself loves you for loving me (C3)
and believing that I came from God.
28 I came from the Father and have come (C1)
into the world
and now I leave the world to go to the Father."

29 His disciples said, "Now you are speaking
30 plainly and not using metaphors! ·Now we
see that you know everything, and do not (C1)
have to wait for questions to be put into
words; because of this we believe that
31 you came from God." ·Jesus answered
them:

141

"Do you believe at last? (C1)
32 Listen; the time will come—in fact it
has come already—
when you will be scattered, each going (C2)
his own way
and leaving me alone.
And yet I am not alone,
because the Father is with me.
33 I have told you all this
so that you may find peace in me.
In the world you will have trouble, (C2)
but be brave:
I have conquered the world."

Week 2 Day 5
Four C's Meditations
on St. John 15:1-16:33

1. Today, Lord, we read the passage where You described Yourself as the true Vine and Your Father as the Vinedresser.*(91)* Basically, You were telling us that we must remain in Your friendship if we are going to bear the fruit of holiness that leads to eternal life in Heaven.

2. We Christians are the branches of the Vine. If we do not bear the fruit of sanctity, the Father cuts us away. Thus we lose contact with the Vine which is the Source of our supernatural, heavenly life. If we bear fruit, however, we will be pruned back by the Father so that we can become even more holy. That is, we will be tested by trials, giving us opportunities to grow in Your love.

3. Although we do not naturally like them, the trials, hardships, sufferings and crosses that come our way are our opportunities for growth in sanctity. If we embrace them with prayer, You, Lord, will give us the grace to endure and conquer them. Each one we successfully overcome makes us a little more like You. And we become more able to love our fellow humans as You, Yourself, love them.

4. If we are never pruned back by the Father, if we never have trials and hardships, if life for us were always easy, how could we really bear the fruit of sanctity, since sanctity comes from leading a life of self-sacrifice in

Your friendship, and in imitation of the way of the Cross? Please, Jesus, give us the grace of constancy so that we can endure and conquer all of life's adversities for Your honor and glory and for the salvation of souls.

5. Jesus, in today's meditation You also said, "If the world hates you, remember that it hated me before you.... Because you do not belong to the world, because my choice withdrew you from the world, therefore the world hates you.... If they persecuted me, they will persecute you too...."(92)

6. Yes, Lord, if we are truly Your consecrated instruments, we must expect to be hated and persecuted by the world, that is, by those who are not in Your friendship, by those who walk in darkness rather than in light.

7. One of the principal reasons the world cannot stand either You or Your followers is because Your life, and the lives of Your followers, stand out in vivid contrast to its own, casting a shadow over the way it lives. Thus, virgins and chaste married people are often ridiculed by those who revel in sexual immorality. Those who abstain from drugs are often reviled, and sometimes assaulted by drug addicts. And those who love You openly, Lord, are often accused of being "holier than thou," and sometimes are even accused of being disloyal to civil governments.

8. Jesus, give us the grace to resist the temptations of the world and to persevere in

faith, hope and seed-charity since the prince of this world and his followers seek to destroy us by luring us away from You. May we always keep in mind St. James' warning that..."making the world your friend is making God your enemy.... Anyone who chooses the world for his friend turns himself into God's enemy."(93)

9. One last thought, Jesus, no sooner had Your Apostles expressed their belief in You as the Messiah sent by God than You prophesied that they would desert You.

10. Lord, we learn from this that having faith is not enough to be Your loyal followers. We must also have seed-charity and constancy with which we will be able to persevere in Your friendship in good times and bad, in times of spiritual tranquility and in times of grave temptations and unrest.

11. "You will be hated by all men on account of my name; but the man who stands firm to the end will be saved."(94)

12. Realistically speaking, however, we know we are weak, Jesus. We often find it difficult to be loyal to You even in relatively tranquil times. How can we really presume that we would not desert You in times of severe temptations or hardships? Yet, Your love and grace are always available to us, as You said to Your servant St. Paul:

13. "The man who thinks that he is safe must be careful that he does not fall. The trials that you have had to bear are no more

than people normally have. You can trust God not to let you be tried beyond your strength, and with any trial he will give you a way out of it and the strength to bear it."(95)

14. "My grace is enough for you. My power is at its best in weakness."(96)

15. Also, St. John records the following words of encouragement which You gave Your Apostles. "In the world You will have trouble, but be brave: I have conquered the world."(97)

16. Most Sacred Heart of Jesus, in the light of our experience of denying You through the weakness and frailty of our sinful wills, please grant us the grace of final perseverance, that special grace received through prayer, so that we can die in Your friendship. And may You strengthen our resolve to please You at all times, even during periods of great trials and difficulties. Amen.

Try to read these Scripture passages and meditations several times a day in a reflective manner. Each time you do so, the Holy Spirit will give you more insights.
Please read and meditate on Chapter IV, Paragraphs 1 to 6 of Peaceful Seed Living, Volume I.

WEEK 2 DAY 6
The Gospel of St. John
Chapters 17:1-18:40

The priestly prayer of Christ

17 After saying this, Jesus raised his eyes to heaven and said:

1 "Father, the hour has come:
 glorify your Son
 so that your Son may glorify you;
2 and, through the power over all mankind*a* that you have given him,
 let him give eternal life to all those you have entrusted to him.
3 And eternal life is this:
 to know you,
 the only true God,
 and Jesus Christ whom you have sent.
4 I have glorified you on earth
 and finished the work
 that you gave me to do.
5 Now, Father, it it time for you to glorify me
 with that glory I had with you
 before ever the world was.
6 I have made your name known

JOHN

    to the men you took from the world to give me.
    They were yours and you gave them to me,
    and they have kept your word. (C4)

7   Now at last they know
    that all you have given me comes indeed from you;
8   for I have given them
    the teaching you gave to me,
    and they have truly accepted this, that (C1)
      I came from you,
    and have believed that it was you who (C1) sent me.

9   I pray for them;
    I am not praying for the world
    but for those you have given me,
    because they belong to you:
10 all I have is yours
    and all you have is mine,
    and in them I am glorified.
11 I am not in the world any longer,
    but they are in the world,
    and I am coming to you.
    Holy Father,
    keep those you have given me true to your name,
    so that they may be one like us.
12 While I was with them,
    I kept those you had given me true to your name.
    I have watched over them and not one is lost
    except the one who chose to be lost,[b] (C1)
    and this was to fulfill the scriptures.
13 But now I am coming to you
    and while still in the world I say these things
    to share my joy with them to the full.
14 I passed your word on to them, (C2)
    and the world hated them,

JOHN

because they belong to the world
no more than I belong to the world.
15 I am not asking you to remove them from the world,
but to protect them from the evil one.
16 They do not belong to the world
any more than I belong to the world.
17 Consecrate them in the truth;
your word is truth.
18 As you sent me into the world,
I have sent them into the world,
19 and for their sake I consecrate myself (c1)
so that they too may be consecrated in (c3) truth.
20 I pray not only for these,
but for those also
who through their words will believe (c1) in me.
21 May they all be one.
Father, may they be one in us,
as you are in me and I am in you, (c1)
so that the world may believe it was you who sent me.
22 I have given them the glory you gave (c3) to me,
that they may be one as we are one. (c4)
23 With me in them and you in me,
may they be so completely one (c3)
that the world will realize that it was (c4) you who sent me
and that I have loved them as much as you loved me.
24 Father,
I want those you have given me
to be with me where I am,
so that they may always see the glory
you have given me
because you loved me
before the foundation of the world.
25 Father, Righteous One,
the world has not known you, (c2)

> but I have known you,
> and these have known
> that you have sent me.
>
> 26 I have made your name known to them
> and will continue to make it known,
> so that the love with which you loved
>   me may be in them, (C3)
> and so that I may be in them." (C4)

C. THE PASSION

The arrest of Jesus

1 **18** After he had said all this Jesus left with his disciples and crossed the Kedron valley. There was a garden there, and he went 2 into it with his disciples. ·Judas the traitor (C2) knew the place well, since Jesus had often 3 met his disciples there, ·and he brought the cohort[a] to this place together with a detach- (C2) ment of guards sent by the chief priests and the Pharisees, all with lanterns and torches 4 and weapons. ·Knowing everything that was going to happen to him, Jesus then came forward and said, "Who are you looking for?" 5 They answered, "Jesus the Nazarene." He (C2) said, "I am he." Now Judas the traitor was 6 standing among them. ·When Jesus said, "I am he," they moved back and fell to the 7 ground. ·He asked them a second time, "Who are you looking for?" They said, 8 "Jesus the Nazarene." ·"I have told you that

I am he," replied Jesus. "If I am the one you
9 are looking for, let these others go." ·This was to fulfill the words he had spoken, "Not one of those you gave me have I lost."

10 Simon Peter, who carried a sword, drew it and wounded the high priest's servant, cutting off his right ear. The servant's name was
11 Malchus. ·Jesus said to Peter, "Put your sword back in its scabbard; am I not to drink the cup that the Father has given me?"

Jesus before Annas and Caiaphas.
Peter disowns him

12 The cohort and its captain and the Jewish (C2)
13 guards seized Jesus and bound him. ·They took him first to Annas, because Annas was the father-in-law of Caiaphas, who was high
14 priest that year. ·It was Caiaphas who had suggested to the Jews, "It is better for one man to die for the people."

15 Simon Peter, with another disciple, followed Jesus. This disciple, who was known to the high priest, went with Jesus into the
16 high priest's palace, ·but Peter stayed outside the door. So the other disciple, the one known to the high priest, went out, spoke to the woman who was keeping the door and
17 brought Peter in. ·The maid on duty at the door said to Peter, "Aren't you another of (C2) that man's disciples?" He answered, "I am
18 not." ·Now it was cold, and the servants and

guards had lit a charcoal fire and were standing there warming themselves; so Peter stood there too, warming himself with the others.

19 The high priest questioned Jesus about his
20 disciples and his teaching. ·Jesus answered, "I have spoken openly for all the world to hear; I have always taught in the synagogue and in the Temple where all the Jews meet
21 together: I have said nothing in secret. ·But why ask me? Ask my hearers what I taught:
22 they know what I said." ·At these words, one of the guards standing by gave Jesus a slap (c2) in the face, saying, "Is that the way to answer
23 the high priest?" ·Jesus replied, "If there is something wrong in what I said, point it out; but if there is no offense in it, why do you (c2)
24 strike me?" ·Then Annas sent him, still bound, to Caiaphas the high priest. (c2)

25 As Simon Peter stood there warming himself, someone said to him, "Aren't you another of his disciples?" He denied it saying,
26 "I am not." ·One of the high priest's servants, (c2) a relation of the man whose ear Peter had cut off, said, "Didn't I see you in the garden with
27 him?" ·Again Peter denied it; and at once a (c2) cock crew.

Jesus before Pilate

28 They then led Jesus from the house of Caiaphas to the Praetorium.^{b} It was now (c2) morning. They did not go into the Praetorium themselves or they would be defiled^c and un-
29 able to eat the Passover. ·So Pilate came outside to them and said, "What charge do you
30 bring against this man?" They replied, ·"If he (c2) were not a criminal, we should not be hand-
31 ing him over to you." ·Pilate said, "Take him yourselves, and try him by your own Law." The Jews answered, "We are not allowed to
32 put a man to death." ·This was to fulfill the **words Jesus had spoken indicating the way he was** going to die.

33 So Pilate went back into the Praetorium and called Jesus to him, "Are you the king 34 of the Jews?" he asked. ·Jesus replied, "Do you ask this of your own accord, or have 35 others spoken to you about me?" ·Pilate answered, "Am I a Jew? It is your own people and the chief priests who have handed you 36 over to me: what have you done?" ·Jesus (C2) replied, "Mine is not a kingdom of this world; if my kingdom were of this world, my men would have fought to prevent my being surrendered to the Jews. But my kingdom is not 37 of this kind." ·"So you are a king then?" said Pilate. "It is you who say it," answered Jesus. "Yes, I am a king. I was born for this, I came into the world for this: to bear witness to the truth; and all who are on the side of truth 38 listen to my voice." ·"Truth?" said Pilate (C1) "What is that?"; and with that he went out (C3) again to the Jews and said, "I find no case 39 against him. ·But according to a custom of yours I should release one prisoner at the Passover; would you like me, then, to release 40 the king of the Jews?" ·At this they shouted: "Not this man," they said, "but Barabbas." Barabbas was a brigand. (C2)

Week 2 Day 6
Four C's Meditations
on St. John 17:1-18:40

1. Jesus, today we began our Scripture reading by meditating on chapter seventeen, which is essentially a priestly prayer in which You consecrated Yourself to the Father on behalf of the Apostles. The chapter also contains a prayer for Church unity. Both prayers describe consecration perfectly and can be summed up in the following four verses.

2. "As you sent me into the world, I have sent them (the Apostles) into the world, and for their sake I consecrate myself so they too may be consecrated in truth. I pray not only for these, but for those also who through their words will believe in me. May they all be one. Father, may they be one in us, as you are in me and I am in you, so that the world may believe it was you who sent me."(98)

3. The first thing that comes to mind, Jesus, is the love You and the Father have for mankind in spite of its sins. "What proves that God loves us is that Christ died for us while we were still sinners."(99) This is particularly striking when we consider our own relations with others. How often we desire to limit our love and concern only to those who are "worthy of it," which often means only to those who have been good to us. But You and the Father have taught us that we are to love even our enemies and those who have deeply hurt us.

4. "Treat others as you would like them to treat you. If you love those who love you, what thanks can you expect? Even sinners love those who love them.... Love your enemies and do good.... You will have a great reward, and you will be sons of the Most High, for he himself is kind to the ungrateful and the wicked."(100)

5. Why do You love sinners, Lord? Not because we deserve it, but because You want us to be like You, full of happiness and love, and possessing eternal life. You sacrificed Yourself to the Father for our sakes so that we could be consecrated in truth, truth which does away with error and leads to Heaven.

6. You consecrated Yourself to the Father so that we humans, divided by sin, might be one with You and with the Father by the grace and power of God the Holy Spirit.

7. Yes, Jesus, You and The Father, together with the Holy Spirit, are not only substantially One but also One in love. One in peace and One in harmony. Indeed, the three Persons of the Holy Trinity constitute the perfect community. In the Trinity, there are no divisions, no hatreds, no evil, no wars. You, Jesus, sacrificed Yourself for us so that we might share in this unity. Because of Your supreme sacrifice for us on the altar of the Cross, we are also given the grace to be one with one another in truth and in love. Thus, through Your Mystical Body the Church, spouses can be permanently united, and families can be united in truth and in love.

Societies can also be united, as can all of mankind. *(See "The Catholic Catechism," pp. 63-67 for a discussion of the Holy Trinity.)*

8. You are the Source of all unity, Lord, and therefore the Healer of all sinful divisions. And to the degree that we allow You to remove our sinfulness, we become united with God and our fellow humans.

9. Too often we fret about the sins of others and neglect our own. But if we are to retain unity with You, and be united within our own beings, we must be primarily concerned with the removal of our own sins and with the sanctification of our souls.

10. "Why do you observe the splinter in your brother's eye and never notice the plank in your own? Hypocrite! Take the plank out of your own eye first, and then you will see clearly enough to take the splinter out of your brother's eye."*(101)*

11. Jesus, we humbly thank You for sacrificing Yourself for us on the Cross. Forgive us our sins and remove them from us

with the power of Your grace. Then we will be able to appropriate for ourselves the merits of Your sacrifice and become one with You, the Father and the Holy Spirit. We will be able to become unified in our souls and unified with our fellow humans. And may the example of our unity with You attract others to find and experience that same unity, whereby they will save their souls and find true and lasting peace.

12. In chapter eighteen, Jesus, we read where St. Peter denied You three times.(102) This must have been extremely painful to You, since You had every right to receive the support of Your Apostles during the time of Your great agony. Peter's denial was particularly distressing since he had earlier promised to lay down his life for You.

13. Peter's example serves as a reminder of the frailty of fallen human nature. Sadly, many of us tend to be like him. During moments when we are free from temptations to sin, it is quite easy to think that we will never betray You again nor rebel against Your Will. But the moment we find ourselves tempted, we too often give in and "betray the innocent blood." But just as St. Peter was given, at Pentecost, an abundance of Your grace, so can we who turn to You receive an abundance of grace to resist and conquer temptation, and become truly holy.(103)

14. Lord, help us to flee from our sins, place You first in our lives, and witness boldly to

You and Your Gospel before our families, friends and acquaintances. Day by day, may we be strengthened in our love for You, and come to that point where we will no longer deny You in our words, thoughts and deeds. Amen.

The very essence of consecration can be found in John 17:13-26. Read it slowly. Reflect on this most powerful prayer of Jesus to His Father. Mark your book and go back to these passages frequently.

Please read and meditate on Chapter V, Paragraphs 1 to 13 of Peaceful Seed Living, Volume I.

WEEK 2 DAY 7
The Gospel of St. John
Chapters 19:1-20:18

19 1 Pilate then had Jesus taken away and (C2) 2 scourged; ·and after this, the soldiers (C2) twisted some thorns into a crown and put it on his head, and dressed him in a purple robe. 3 They kept coming up to him and saying, (C2) "Hail, king of the Jews!"; and they slapped him in the face. (C2)
4   Pilate came outside again and said to them, "Look, I am going to bring him out to you 5 to let you see that I find no case." ·Jesus then came out wearing the crown of thorns and the purple robe. Pilate said, "Here is the man."
6 When they saw him the chief priests and the guards shouted, "Crucify him! Crucify him!" (C2) Pilate said, "Take him yourselves and crucify him: I can find no case against him."
7 "We have a Law," the Jews replied, "and according to that Law he ought to die, because he has claimed to be the Son of God."
8   When Pilate heard them say this his fears 9 increased. ·Reentering the Praetorium, he

JOHN

said to Jesus, "Where do you come from?"
10 But Jesus made no answer. •Pilate then said to him, "Are you refusing to speak to me? Surely you know I have power to release you
11 and I have power to crucify you?" •"You would have no power over me," replied Jesus, "if it had not been given to you from above; that is why the one who handed me over to you has the greater guilt."

Jesus is condemned to death

12 From that moment Pilate was anxious to set him free, but the Jews shouted, "If you set him free you are no friend of Caesar's; anyone who makes himself king is defying
13 Caesar." •Hearing these words, Pilate had Jesus brought out, and seated himself on the chair of judgment at a place called the Pave-
14 ment, in Hebrew Gabbatha. •It was Passover Preparation Day, about the sixth hour.*a* "Here is your king," said Pilate to the Jews.
15 "Take him away, take him away!" they said. "Crucify him!" "Do you want me to crucify your king?" said Pilate. The chief priests answered, "We have no king except Caesar."
16 So in the end Pilate handed him over to them to be crucified.

The crucifixion

17 They then took charge of Jesus, •and carrying his own cross he went out of the city to the place of the skull or, as it was called in
18 Hebrew, Golgotha, •where they crucified him with two others, one on either side with Jesus
19 in the middle. •Pilate wrote out a notice and had it fixed to the cross; it ran: "Jesus the
20 Nazarene, King of the Jews." •This notice was read by many of the Jews, because the place where Jesus was crucified was not far from the city, and the writing was in Hebrew,
21 Latin and Greek. •So the Jewish chief priests

JOHN

said to Pilate, "You should not write 'King of the Jews,' but 'This man said: I am King of the Jews.' " •Pilate answered, "What I have written, I have written."

Christ's garments divided

23 When the soldiers had finished crucifying Jesus they took his clothing and divided it into four shares, one for each soldier. His undergarment was seamless, woven in one piece from neck to hem; •so they said to one another, "Instead of tearing it, let's throw dice to decide who is to have it." In this way the words of scripture were fulfilled:

They shared out my clothing among them.
They cast lots for my clothes.[b]

This is exactly what the soldiers did.

Jesus and his mother

25 Near the cross of Jesus stood his mother and his mother's sister, Mary the wife of Clopas, and Mary of Magdala. •Seeing his mother and the disciple he loved standing near her, Jesus said to his mother, "Woman, (c3) this is your son." •Then to the disciple he said, "This is your mother." And from that moment the disciple made a place for her in (c3) his home.

The death of Jesus

28 After this, Jesus knew that everything had now been completed, and to fulfill the scripture perfectly he said:

"I am thirsty."[c]

29 A jar full of vinegar stood there, so putting a sponge soaked in the vinegar on a hyssop stick they held it up to his mouth. •After Jesus had taken the vinegar he said, "It is accom-

plished;" and bowing his head he gave up his spirit.

The pierced Christ

31 It was Preparation Day, and to prevent the bodies remaining on the cross during the sabbath—since that sabbath was a day of special solemnity—the Jews asked Pilate to have the legs broken[d] and the bodies taken away.
32 Consequently the soldiers came and broke the legs of the first man who had been cruci-
33 fied with him and then of the other. ·When they came to Jesus, they found he was already dead, and so instead of breaking his
34 legs ·one of the soldiers pierced his side with a lance; and immediately there came out
35 blood and water. ·This is the evidence of one who saw it—trustworthy evidence, and he knows he speaks the truth—and he gives it
36 so that you may believe as well. ·Because all this happened to fulfill the words of scripture:

Not one bone of his will be broken;[e]

37 and again, in another place scripture says:

They will look on the one whom they have pierced.[f]

c. Ps 22:15 d. To hasten death. e. Two texts are here combined: Ps 34:20 and Ex 12:46. The allusion is both to God protecting the good man, and to the ritual for preparing the Passover lamb. f. Zc 12:10

The burial

38 After this, Joseph of Arimathaea, who was a disciple of Jesus—though a secret one because he was afraid of the Jews—asked Pilate to let him remove the body of Jesus. Pilate gave permission, so they came and took it 39 away. •Nicodemus came as well—the same one who had first come to Jesus at nighttime—and he brought a mixture of myrrh and aloes, weighing about a hundred pounds. 40 They took the body of Jesus and wrapped it with the spices in linen cloths, following the 41 Jewish burial customs. •At the place where he had been crucified there was a garden, and in this garden a new tomb in which no one 42 had yet been buried. •Since it was the Jewish Day of Preparation and the tomb was near at hand, they laid Jesus there.

VIII. THE DAY OF CHRIST'S RESURRECTION

The empty tomb

1 **20** It was very early on the first day of the week and still dark, when Mary of Magdala came to the tomb. She saw that the stone had been moved away from the tomb 2 and came running to Simon Peter and the

JOHN

other disciple, the one Jesus loved. "They have taken the Lord out of the tomb," she said, "and we don't know where they have put him."

3 So Peter set out with the other disciple to
4 go to the tomb. ·They ran together, but the other disciple, running faster than Peter,
5 reached the tomb first; ·he bent down and saw the linen cloths lying on the ground, but
6 did not go in. ·Simon Peter who was following now came up, went right into the tomb,
7 saw the linen cloths on the ground, ·and also the cloth that had been over his head; this was not with the linen cloths but rolled up in a
8 place by itself. ·Then the other disciple who had reached the tomb first also went in; he (C1)
9 saw and he believed. ·Till this moment they had failed to understand the teaching of scrip-
10 ture, that he must rise from the dead. ·The disciples then went home again.

The appearance to Mary of Magdala

11 Meanwhile Mary stayed outside near the (C3) tomb, weeping. Then, still weeping, she
12 stooped to look inside, ·and saw two angels in white sitting where the body of Jesus had been, one at the head, the other at the feet.
13 They said, "Woman, why are you weeping?" "They have taken my Lord away," she replied, "and I don't know where they have put
14 him." ·As she said this she turned round and saw Jesus standing there, though she did not
15 recognize him. ·Jesus said, "Woman, why are you weeping? Who are you looking for?" Supposing him to be the gardener, she said, "Sir, if you have taken him away, tell me where you have put him, and I will go and
16 remove him." ·Jesus said, "Mary!" She knew him then and said to him in Hebrew, "Rab-
17 buni!"—which means Master. ·Jesus said to her, "Do not cling to me, because I have not

yet ascended to the Father. But go and find the brothers, and tell them: I am ascending to my Father and your Father, to my God
18 and your God." •So Mary of Magdala went and told the disciples that she had seen the (c3) Lord and that he had said these things to her.

Week 2 Day 7
Four C's Meditations
on St. John 19:1-20:18

1. Yesterday, Jesus, we meditated on Peter's weakness. Today, we reflected on the frailty of Pontius Pilate.*(104)* Pilate was a man who acted against his conscience in order to achieve a momentary peace; a false peace that comes from conforming to the world. Concretely speaking, Pilate refused to free You, Lord, not because he thought You were guilty of a crime, but because he wanted the approval of the crowds that demanded Your death.

2. We, too, are guilty at times of behaving like Pilate. When acquaintances or friends, for instance, are being slandered or gossiped about, we often keep our mouths shut or, even worse, add to the sin instead of defending them in charity.

3. We are reminded of an incident that occured in the army several years ago. A platoon leader was forcing one of his men to drink beer because the soldier had expressed his belief that it was unchristian to consume alcoholic beverages. Out of the sixty or so men witnessing the incident not one came to the poor man's defense, although the injustice and cruelty involved in the situation were evident to all. (The point here, of course, is not that drinking alcohol, as such, is wrong, but that a person was forced to act against his conscience, and no one came to his rescue.

For an informative presentation on conscience, read pp. 290-295 of "The Catholic Catechism.")

4. Lord, how much, at times, we love ourselves and the ways of the world more than we love You. And how foolish! You alone can give us true happiness, joy and peace. Yet we turn from You and do the very things that may lead us to everlasting hell. Please help us to see the folly of our conformity to the world, and inspire us always to place You and Your will for us first in our lives.

5. Next, Merciful Savior, St. John gave us an account of Your Crucifixion. Actually,

Your sacred death should be meditated on over and over again, during the course of our lives, so that we can constantly recall and receive insights into the mystery of Your unsurpassed love for us.

6. "A man can have no greater love than to lay down his life for his friends."*(105)*

7. "But what proves that God loves us is that Christ died for us while we were still sinners."*(106)*

8. Yes, Lord, the Crucifixion itself manifested Your generous love, but so did Your words spoken from the Cross. There You were, dying in agony, yet You continued to be mindful of the needs of others till the bitter end. This was evident, for example, when You commended Your Blessed Mother to St. John's safe-keeping. And Your love was also seen when You pleaded with the Father to forgive those who crucified You, since they did not fully realize the enormity of their crime.*(107)*

9. Thankfully, Lord, You have given us not only Your example of self-sacrificing love, but also the very love itself which we possess when we are in Your friendship. May we use it daily to imitate You and Your saints, and to help bring souls into Your Kingdom of Heaven.

10. We also noted in today's lesson Your disciple, St. Joseph of Arimathaea, who mystically representing Your foster father, St. Joseph, provided for Your needs by

devoutly taking Your Sacred Body and burying it in his tomb. This incident serves as a reminder that we should treat Your Eucharistic Body with great respect and devotion, whether at Mass, or Benediction, or when it is present in church tabernacles. Moreover, we should treat Your Mystical Body, the Church, with sacrificial love and devotion, as well as those who are its members. "While we have a chance, we must do good to all, especially to our brothers in the faith."*(108) (For a discussion on the Eucharist and the Eucharistic Presence, see "The Catholic Catechism," pp. 458-465;479-480.)*

11. In chapter twenty, Jesus, St. John tells us of events involving Your bodily Resurrection from the dead. It is this miracle, above all others, that points to You as the Messiah and substantiates Your doctrines. *(For a discussion on the value of miracles as signs supporting the truths of Faith, see "The Catholic Catechism," p. 38.)*

12. It is not surprising, then, that from the time of the Apostles there have always been

those who have denied the Resurrection, not on the basis of solid evidence, but because it conflicted with their philosophical or religious points of view. This attitude is seen, for example, in St. Matthew's Gospel, where we are told that the chief priests and elders of the Jews, upon learning of the empty tomb, which pointed to Your Resurrection and Messiahship, bribed soldiers to say that Your disciples had stolen Your Body.*(109)*

13. Thank You, Jesus, for Your Apostles who risked their lives, and endured great hardships over a period of many years, insisting that You, having conquered sin and death, were raised bodily from the dead.*(110)* Strengthen our faith in this great mystery and may we refer to it often when we try to help others accept You as the Messiah sent by God the Father to redeem mankind.

Try to read these Scripture passages and meditations several times a day in a reflective manner. Each time you do so, the Holy Spirit will give you more insights.

Please read and meditate on Chapter V, Paragraphs 14 to 30 of Peaceful Seed Living, Volume I.

WEEK 3 DAY 1
The Gospel of St. John
Chapter 20:19-21:25

Appearances to the disciples

19 In the evening of that same day, the first day of the week, the doors were closed in the room where the disciples were, for fear of the Jews. Jesus came and stood among them. He
20 said to them, "Peace be with you," ·and showed them his hands and his side. The disciples were filled with joy when they saw
21 the Lord, ·and he said to them again, "Peace be with you.

"As the Father sent me,
so am I sending you."

22 After saying this he breathed on them·and said:

"Receive the Holy Spirit.
23   For those whose sins you forgive,
         they are forgiven;
         for those whose sins you retain,
         they are retained."

24 Thomas, called the Twin, who was one of the Twelve, was not with them when Jesus
25 came. ·When the disciples said, "We have seen the Lord," he answered, "Unless I see the holes that the nails made in his hands and can put my finger into the holes they made, and unless I can put my hand into his side, (C2)
26 I refuse to believe." ·Eight days later the disciples were in the house again and Thomas was with them. The doors were closed, but Jesus came in and stood among them. "Peace
27 be with you," he said. ·Then he spoke to Thomas, "Put your finger here; look, here are my hands. Give me your hand; put it into my
28 side. Doubt no longer but believe." ·Thomas (C1)
29 replied, "My Lord and my God!" ·Jesus said

170

to him:

"You believe because you can see me.
Happy are those who have not seen and yet (c1)
believe."

CONCLUSION

30 There were many other signs that Jesus worked and the disciples saw, but they are
31 not recorded in this book. ·These are recorded so that you may believe that Jesus is the Christ, the Son of God, and that believing this you may have life through his name.

APPENDIX[a]

The appearance on the shore of Tiberias

1 **21** Later on, Jesus showed himself again to the disciples. It was by the Sea of
2 Tiberias, and it happened like this: ·Simon Peter, Thomas called the Twin, Nathanael from Cana in Galilee, the sons of Zebedee and two more of his disciples were together.
3 Simon Peter said, "I'm going fishing." They replied, "We'll come with you." They went out and got into the boat but caught nothing that night.

4 It was light by now and there stood Jesus on the shore, though the disciples did not
5 realize that it was Jesus. ·Jesus called out, "Have you caught anything, friends?" And
6 when they answered, "No," ·he said, "Throw the net out to starboard and you'll find something." So they dropped the net, and there were so many fish that they could not haul
7 it in. ·The disciple Jesus loved said to Peter, "It is the Lord." At these words, "It is the Lord," Simon Peter, who had practically nothing on, wrapped his cloak round him and
8 jumped into the water. ·The other disciples

came on in the boat, towing the net and the fish; they were only about a hundred yards from land.

9 As soon as they came ashore they saw that there was some bread there, and a charcoal
10 fire with fish cooking on it. ·Jesus said, "Bring some of the fish you have just
11 caught." ·Simon Peter went aboard and dragged the net to the shore, full of big fish, one hundred and fifty-three of them; and in spite of there being so many the net was not
12 broken. ·Jesus said to them, "Come and have breakfast." None of the disciples was bold enough to ask, "Who are you?"; they knew
13 quite well it was the Lord. ·Jesus then stepped forward, took the bread and gave it
14 to them, and the same with the fish. ·This was the third time that Jesus showed himself to the disciples after rising from the dead.

15 After the meal Jesus said to Simon Peter, (C3) "Simon son of John, do you love me more than these others do?" He answered, "Yes (C3) Lord, you know I love you." Jesus said to
16 him, "Feed my lambs." ·A second time he said to him, "Simon son of John, do you love (C3) me?" He replied, "Yes, Lord, you know I (C3) love you." Jesus said to him, "Look after my
17 sheep." ·Then he said to him a third time, (C3) "Simon son of John, do you love me?" Peter

JOHN

was upset that he asked him the third time, (C3)
"Do you love me?" and said, "Lord, you
know everything; you know I love you." (C3)
Jesus said to him, "Feed my sheep.

18 "I tell you most solemnly,
when you were young
you put on your own belt
and walked where you liked;
but when you grow old
you will stretch out your hands,
and somebody else will put a belt round you (C2)
and take you where you would rather not
   go."

19 In these words he indicated the kind of death
by which Peter would give glory to God. (C3)
After this he said, "Follow me." (C4)
20 Peter turned and saw the disciple Jesus (C3)
loved following them—the one who had
leaned on his breast at the supper and had
said to him, "Lord, who is it that will betray
21 you?" ·Seeing him, Peter said to Jesus,
22 "What about him, Lord?" ·Jesus answered,
"If I want him to stay behind till I come, what
does it matter to you? You are to follow
23 me." ·The rumor then went out among the
brothers that this disciple would not die. Yet
Jesus had not said to Peter, "He will not die,"
but, "If I want him to stay behind till I
come."

Conclusion

24 This disciple is the one who vouches for
these things and has written them down, and
we know that his testimony is true.
25 There were many other things that Jesus
did; if all were written down, the world itself,
I suppose, would not hold all the books that
would have to be written.

Week 3 Day 1
Four C's Meditations
on St. John 20:19-21:25

1. Lord, in the closing passages of St. John's Gospel, we discovered that You made several appearances to Your disciples after Your Resurrection. In one, You appeared to them as they were gathered in a room behind closed doors. You showed them Your pierced hands and side, demonstrating that You were not simply a phantom.

2. At this time, You twice said to them, "Peace be with you,"*(111)* indicating Your love for them. You wanted them to experience spiritual peace in spite of the trials and hardships awaiting them.*(112)* Lord, You call us also to experience Your peace, but in this life it must be accompanied as well by the crosses You ask us to bear daily.*(113)* At first glance this might seem like a contradiction, but, in fact, it is not.

174

3. That deeply satisfying spiritual peace we all desire comes only from doing Your Will. But in this life, conforming to Your will often involves suffering. This is so because we must combat evil and temptations to evil whether they come from within or without. Our vices, for instance, can only be conquered through grace, prayers and stubborn resistance to temptation. And to the degree that we conquer them, we experience Your peace. Or we can suffer in defense of the Faith, as many are doing today, and also experience Your peace. We got a glimmer of this truth, Lord, when we read how Your Apostles suffered at the hands of the Jewish Council (the Sanhedrin) in Jerusalem.

4. "...they had the apostles called in, gave orders for them to be flogged, warned them not to speak in the name of Jesus and released them. And so they left the presence of the Sanhedrin glad to have had the honor of suffering humiliation for the sake of the name."*(114)*

5. Jesus, may Your peace always rule our hearts.

6. Returning to our meditation in John's Gospel, Lord, You said a second time, "Peace be with you." Then You exclaimed, "As the Father sent me, so am I sending you...."*(115)*

7. As You have been sent by the Father as an act of charity to save us from our sins and save us for life in Heaven, so You sent Your Apostles into the world in charity to represent You, and to bring the nations into Your Mystical Body, the Church.

8. Next, You breathed on them, saying, "Receive the Holy Spirit. For those whose sins you forgive, they are forgiven; for those whose sins you retain they are retained."*(116)* Thus, You gave the Apostles the power to forgive sins in Your Name, Lord. What an act of love! And how fortunate are the millions who over the centuries have received the forgiveness of their sins through the sacrament of Penance, which You entrusted to the authority and priestly power of the Apostles.

9. St. John also shares with us, in today's reading, the account of Your post-Resurrection appearance to the "Doubting Apostle," St. Thomas. At first, doubting it was You, he thrust his hands into Your wounds, Lord. He then believed, and accepted the fact You had risen bodily from the dead.*(117)* Here we have another piece of historical evidence supporting the Resurrection, yet there are those who continue either to doubt or deny this doctrine

which comes to us from the Apostles.

10. We noted also, Jesus, that St. Thomas acknowledged You to be divine when he cried out, "My Lord, and my God!"*(118)* Nonetheless, there exist "Christians," today, who, unlike Thomas, refuse to believe in Your divinity. But, Jesus, we know that they don't base their denials on historical or scientific evidence. Rather these negations are founded on a sort of negative blind faith in false assumptions such as "miracles cannot exist," and "God would not or could not become man." Consequently, these people maintain that the Resurrection accounts in the New Testament are not true and therefore not based on anything that really happened. Rather they are, it is maintained, fictional stories calculated to support the faith of simple, supersititious people.

11. We, on the other hand, Lord, accept the historical reality of the Resurrection to which the Apostles testified, in spite of their imprisonments, beatings, persecutions and martyrdoms. Lord, we believe in Your Resurrection, but please help us to overcome temptations to doubt. And we pray that those who doubt or deny this doctrine may be converted to the truth.

12. Finally, Lord Jesus, we spent some time reflecting on Your post-Resurrection appearance to St. Peter.*(119)* Here You gave him the opportunity to undo his three-fold denial by a three-fold affirmation of his love for You. After each affirmation You told him

to look after Your sheep, that is, to look after the People of God who constitute the Church.

13. This passage, Lord, reminds us of two others in which You singled out Peter from the other Apostles. In one You told him that You had prayed that he would have an unfailing faith so that he could strengthen the faith of his brother Apostles.*(120)* In the other, You said to Peter, whose real name was Simon the son of John, "You are Peter (*Kepha*) and on this rock (*Kepha*) I will build my church."*(121)* In other words, You said to Peter "Simon, I'm going to call you Peter, or Rock, and upon this Rock, I will build my Church." Moreover, Jesus, You promised him the authority to govern it in Your holy Name.*(122)*(*Kepha* is the Aramaic word for Peter and Rock which Jesus actually spoke.)

178

14. Lord, forgive us for the many times we have denied You and have prevented Your influence in our lives, and in the lives of others, because of our scandalous behavior. May we make amends and beome strengthened in our faith and love for You and in our love for others. And may Peter's example of recovery to Your friendship and grace always serve as a sign of encouragement and hope for us in moments of weakness. Amen.

Try to read these Scripture passages and meditations several times a day in a reflective manner. Each time you do so, the Holy Spirit will give you more insights.

Please read and meditate on Chapter VI, Paragraphs 1 to 20 of Peaceful Seed Living, Volume I.

WEEK 3 DAY 2
The First Letter of St. John
Chapter 1:1-2:11

1 John

THE FIRST LETTER OF JOHN

INTRODUCTION

The incarnate Word

1 1 Something which has existed since the beginning,
that we have heard,
and we have seen with our own eyes;
that we have watched
and touched with our hands:
the Word, who is life—
this is our subject.

2 That life was made visible: (C1)
we saw it and we are giving our testimony, (C3)
telling you of the eternal life
which was with the Father and has been made visible to us.

3 What we have seen and heard

we are telling you (C3)
so that you too may be in union with us,
as we are in union (C3)
with the Father (C1)
and with his Son Jesus Christ. (C2)

4 We are writing this to you to make our
own joy complete. (C3)

1 JOHN

I. WALK IN THE LIGHT

5 This is what we have heard from him,
and the message that we are announcing
to you: (C3)
God is light; there is no darkness in him
at all.

6 If we say that we are in union with God*
while we are living in darkness, (C2)
we are lying because we are not living the (C2)
truth.

7 But if we live our lives in the light, (C3)
as he is in the light,
we are in union with one another,
and the blood of Jesus, his Son, (C3)
purifies us from all sin. (C2)

First condition: break with sin

8 If we say we have no sin in us, (C2)
we are deceiving ourselves
and refusing to admit the truth;

9 but if we acknowledge our sins, (C3)
then God who is faithful and just (C2)
will forgive our sins and purify us (C2)
from everything that is wrong.

10 To say that we have never sinned
is to call God a liar (C2)
and to show that his word is not in us.

2 I am writing this, my children,
to stop you sinning; (C2)
but if anyone should sin, (C2)
we have our advocate with the Father,
Jesus Christ, who is just;

2 he is the sacrifice that takes our sins away,
and not only ours,
but the whole world's.

**Second condition: keep the commandments,
especially the law of love**

3 We can be sure that we know God
  only by keeping his commandments. (C3)
4 Anyone who says, "I know him,"
  and does not keep his commandments, (C2)
  is a liar,
  refusing to admit the truth. (C2)
5 But when anyone does obey what he has said,
  God's love comes to perfection in him. (C3)
  We can be sure
  that we are in God
6 only when the one who claims to be living in him
  is living the same kind of life as Christ (C3)
  lived.
7 My dear people, (C4)
  this is not a new commandment that I am writing to tell you,
  but an old commandment
  that you were given from the beginning,
  the original commandment which was the message brought to you.
8 Yet in another way, what I am writing to you,
  and what is being carried out in your lives as it was in his,
  is a new commandment;
  because the night is over

and the real light is already shining.
9 Anyone who claims to be in the light (C2)
but hates his brother
is still in the dark.
10 But anyone who loves his brother is living (C3)
in the light
and need not be afraid of stumbling;
unlike the man who hates his brother and
is in the darkness, (C2)
11 not knowing where he is going,
because it is too dark to see.

Week 3 Day 2
Four C's Meditations
on 1 John 1:1-2:11

1. Jesus, our divine Savior, today we meditated on St. John's First Letter which, as You know, was written as a means of implementing Your commandment to make disciples of all peoples.*(123)* We also learned that John wrote it as an act of Christian love for his intended readers since he desired that they enjoy Christian unity, a unity actuated by seed-charity.

2. "What we have seen and heard we are telling you so that you too may be in union with us, as we are in unity with the Father and his Son Jesus Christ. We are writing this to you to make our own joy complete."*(124)*

3. We too, Jesus, as Your disciples, are called to share with others our communion with You and the Father, a communion brought about by God the Holy Spirit. Therefore, inspire us continuously to draw those who do not now love You into full communion with You in Your Catholic Church.

4. Jesus, in today's Scripture lesson, St. John also wrote:

5. "If we say we have no sin in us, we are deceiving ourselves and refusing to admit the truth; but if we acknowledge our sins, then God who is faithful and just will forgive our sins and purify us from everything that is wrong. To say that we have never sinned is to call God a liar and to show that his word is not in us."*(125)*

6. For some it may seem hard to believe that there are Christians who do not believe they are sinners. But, in fact, they do exist. Many of them do not lead scandalous lives, and certainly not lives of crime. But it is this very fact that presents the greatest problem for them, since they tend to identify sin only with scandalous acts and with crime. Therefore, things such as malicious gossip, envy, greed, failure to pray and to worship God from the heart, and conceit and pride,

are not seen as sinful. And since they do not see themselves as sinners, they cannot really call You their Savior.

7. Lord, here then is where we could be of assistance. If we have children, for example, who think this way we could point out very clearly to them the nature of sin, stressing the fact that it is found in those thoughts, words and actions which counter Your will for us. Next, we could note concrete examples of sins, especially those which are not crimes, and are not generally regarded as horrendous; sins such as laziness, gluttony and envy.

8. For those who really believe they have no need for divine forgiveness, the following portion of Psalm 14 might help.

9. "Their deeds are corrupt and vile, there is not one good man left. Yahweh (God) is looking down from heaven on the sons of men, to see if a single one is wise, if a single one is seeking God. All have turned aside, all alike are tainted; there is not one good man left, not a single one." And then there is that well-known saying in the Letter to the Hebrews in which You, Jesus, are said to be just like us except for sin.

10. "For it is not as if we have a high priest incapable of feeling our weaknesses with us; but we have one who had been tempted in every way that we are, though he is without sin."*(126)* Finally, St. Paul made crystal clear the fact that we are all sinners.

11. "Well then, sin entered the world through one man, and through sin death, and thus sin has spread through the whole human race because everyone has sinned."*(127)*

12. Jesus, inspire us to examine our consciences daily in the light of Your teaching. And may we always honestly and humbly acknowledge and confess our sins, so that we can receive Your divine forgiveness and begin life anew in Your presence, and with the aid of Your grace.

13. Lord, St. John said that we can be sure that we are living in God only when we lead the same type of life that You led while on earth.*(128)* Basically, this means that we must be leading a life of self-sacrificing love, where we place Your divine will above our own. In doing so, we will have communion with God the Father, and with all who love and do His will. This does not mean, of course, that to be in communion with God we must have no sin in us at all. But, whatever sins we do have must not be serious enough to prevent God's love from operating in us. In other words, our sins must be no more than venial, so that our

love for God and His will will not have ceased to be the primary motivating force in our lives. *(For a discussion of venial sin, see "The Catholic Catechism," pp. 183-184.)*

14. Jesus, St. John gives us another test of whether or not we are living in God's friendship. He writes that if we love our brother, we are "in the light," but he who hates his brother is still "in the darkness."*(129)* But as we have mentioned elsewhere in these meditations, we cannot really love our brother with the grace of seed-charity unless we first love God. By loving God, the Father, the Son and the Holy Spirit, first and foremost, we are given the seed-charity we need to love our neighbor as ourselves, and to love him in the same manner as You loved us, Lord. We are given the Light to see and love You in every person that comes into our lives.

15. Most holy Father, may we always love You above all things, and our neighbors as ourselves. This we ask in the Name of Jesus Christ Your Son, Whom with You and the Holy Spirit are God forever. Amen.

Try to read these Scripture passages and meditations several times a day in a reflective manner. Each time you do so, the Holy Spirit will give you more insights.

Please read and meditate on Chapter VI, Paragraphs 21 to 28 of Peaceful Seed Living, Volume I.

WEEK 3 DAY 3
The First Letter of St. John
Chapter 2:12-29

Third condition: detachment from the world

12 I am writing to you, my own children, (C2)
 whose sins have already been forgiven
  through his name;
13 I am writing to you, fathers,
 who have come to know the one (C1)
 who has existed since the beginning; (C3)
 I am writing to you, young men, (C3)
 who have already overcome the Evil One;
14 I have written to you, children, (C1)
 because you already know the Father; (C3)
 I have written to you, fathers, (C1)
 because you have come to know the one
 who has existed since the beginning; (C3)
 I have written to you, young men,
 because you are strong and God's word
  has made its home in you, (C1)
 and you have overcome the Evil One. (C3)
15 You must not love this passing world (C2)
 or anything that is in the world. (C3)
 The love of the Father cannot be
 in any man who loves the world, (C2)

16 because nothing the world has to offer
—the sensual body, (C2)
the lustful eye, (C2)
pride in possessions— (C2)
could ever come from the Father
but only from the world;
17 and the world, with all it craves for, (C2)
is coming to an end;
but anyone who does the will of God (C3)
remains for ever.

Fourth condition: be on guard against the enemies of Christ

18 Children, these are the last days;
you were told that an Antichrist must come, (C2)
and now several antichrists have already appeared;
we know from this that these are the last days.
19 Those rivals of Christ came out of our (C2)
own number, but they had never really belonged;
if they had belonged, they would have (C2)
stayed with us;
but they left us, to prove that not one of them
ever belonged to us.
20 But you have been anointed by the Holy One,
and have all received the knowledge.

1 JOHN

21 It is not because you do not know the truth that I am writing to you
  but rather because you know it already (C1)
  and know that no lie can come from the truth. (C2)
22 The man who denies that Jesus is the Christ— (C2)
  he is the liar,
  he is Antichrist; (C2)
  and he is denying the Father as well as the Son, (C2)
23 because no one who has the Father can deny the Son,
  and to acknowledge the Son is to have the Father as well. (C2) (C1)
24 Keep alive in yourselves what you were taught in the beginning: (C1) (C4)
  as long as what you were taught in the beginning is alive in you, (C3)
  you will live in the Son
  and in the Father;
25 and what is promised to you by his own promise
  is eternal life.
26 This is all that I am writing to you about the people who are trying to lead you astray. (C2)
27 But you have not lost the anointing that he gave you,
  and you do not need anyone to teach you;
  the anointing he gave teaches you everything;
  you are anointed with truth, not with a lie, (C2)
  and as it has taught you, so you must stay in him. (C4)
28 Live in Christ, then, my children,
  so that if he appears, we may have full confidence, (C1)
  and not turn from him in shame (C2)
  at his coming.

1 JOHN

29 You know that God is righteous—
    then you must recognize that everyone
        whose life is righteous (C3)
    has been begotten by him.

Week 3 Day 3
Four C's Meditations
on I John 2:12-29

1. Jesus, in today's meditation, we dwelt on St. John's warning against loving the world and all it has to offer.

2. "You must not love this passing world or anything that is in the world."*(130)* We realize that we remarked about this before when we noted that the "world," used in this sense, referred not to creation as such, but only that aspect of it which is divorced from, and opposed to, God and the Gospel. But St. John introduces a new element here, namely, that we are not to love "the passing world" or

anything in it. At first sight, it might appear that he actually meant that the material world, made by You, was sinful. But this is really not so as we learn from St. John himself.

3. "...nothing the world has to offer - the sensual body, the lustful eye, pride in possessions - could ever come from the Father but only from the world...."*(131)* Another translation of the passage speaks of the worldly offerings of "...the lust of the flesh, and the lust of the eyes and the pride of life."

4. It is these sinful things that St. John meant by "things in the world." And it is these, together with everything sinful, that constitute "this passing world." It is these that draw our hearts away from You, Jesus. The lust of the flesh seeks to make pleasure its god. Pleasure, then, becomes an end in itself. Logically, therefore, anything that would produce pleasure, no matter how vile, would be regarded as acceptable.

5. The lust of the eyes usually refers to greed. It deals with the passionate longing for unnecessary material goods and wealth. The pride of life, which is perhaps a better translation than "pride in possessions," has to do with an uncontrolled desire for worldly honors and attention. A person who ambitiously seeks honors, awards, self-glory, public acclaim and admiration is suffering from this evil.

6. Lord, Jesus, we are so weak. Protect us always from the lust of the flesh, the lust of the

eyes, from the pride of life. May we seek only Your honor and glory so that You may increase and we may decrease.(132) Thus, it will be no longer us but You Who rule our hearts.

7. Jesus, St. John wrote that during the "last days"* there would be antichrists, or those who oppose You and to the truth You came to give us for our salvation. Indeed, today, there is a whole multitude of antichrists. Some of them are openly non-Christian such as those who spread atheistic Marxism.** Others label themselves as Christians but deliberately misrepresent Your teaching as contained in traditional Christianity. (*The "last days" referred to here is the last period of world history which began with the Crucifixion and Resurrection.)

(**Marxism is sometimes thought of as a "Christian" heresy since it developed within a Christian culture. But unlike the early heresies it rejects all supernatural realities.)

8. Volumes have been written on these antichrists and their doctrines, so we could not possibly deal with all of them in this brief meditation. Nonetheless, two of the more important beliefs proclaimed by some antichrists might be at least mentioned. One claims that You, Jesus, were only a man, a man among men; a good man, perhaps, but only a man. The other holds that in the area of morality there are no absolutes. Whatever is moral and good is determined entirely by

individual motives and circumstances, not by an unchanging moral law designed to govern an unchanging human nature created by God. Morality then, according to this view, is only relative.

9. The assertion that You, Jesus, are (were) only a man flies in the face of the unambiguous teaching of the Apostles, which has been handed down to us over the centuries through the Church and is found in the Bible. If You were only a man, You would never be our Savior, in the sense that You take away our sins and make it possible for us to share in Your divine nature for all eternity. Only a divine Being such as Yourself could acomplish this. No mere man, no matter how good he may be, could ever save himself from his sinful condition, let alone the sinful condition of the rest of mankind. Nor could he restore the gift of bodily immortality to humanity.

10. To maintain that morality is only relative defies reason and scientific analysis, as You well know, Lord, better than anyone else. All visible creatures have a common nature,

according to their species, and they are required to conform to the laws governing them. Otherwise they would cease to act according to their particular nature and bring disorder to themselves. Dogs, for example, which failed to behave as dogs would soon die or become insane. Corn which did not act as corn would create problems for farmers and perhaps human consumers. And humans who do not behave as human beings, that is, do not conform to their human nature, perform unnatural acts.

11. If there were no such thing as a common human nature, subject to absolute norms of behavior, there would be no such thing as humanity. In other words, if what once was human changed fundamentally, it would obviously no longer be human, even if it were still labeled as such. And if, as some maintain, each "human" is an entity unto himself, subject to his own laws of behavior, then there would be no such thing as humanity. There would be only billions of individual species, all of which were falsely labeled human, with the possible exception of one.

And if this were so it would be cruel to have laws against murder, theft, excessive speeding, adultery, fornication, mugging, etc., since what was wrong for one "human" might not be wrong for another.

12. In the realm of salvation, Lord, if there is no common human nature subject to absolute laws of behavior, then You could not have assumed such a nature in order to redeem it. Thus You would not and could not be the Savior of mankind. Or if "human" nature were constantly changing, You at most could have redeemed only the "human" nature that existed two thousand years ago, and not this entirely new "human" nature that exists today but will cease to exist tomorrow.

13. Lord, "What fools these mortals be!"* Jesus, protect us against the antichrists of our own day who seek to drive us from the sure path of salvation which You revealed to us while on earth. For those who do not know, help them to discover what the Apostles taught and passed on to succeeding generations in Your Church. Amen.**
(*Shakespeare, "A Midsummer's Night's Dream", Act 3, Scene 2.) *(**For a summary of the teaching of the Apostolic Church consult "The Catholic Catechism" in its entirety.)*

Try to read these Scripture passages and meditations several times a day in a reflective manner. Each time you do so, the Holy Spirit will give you more insights.

Please read and meditate on Chapter VII and Chapter VIII, James 1 verses 1 to 27 of Peaceful Seed Living, Volume I.

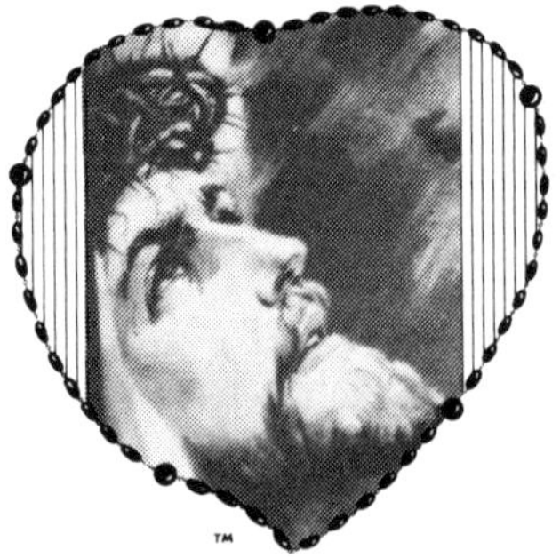

WEEK 3 DAY 4
The First Letter of St. John
Chapters 3:1-4:8

II. LIVE AS GOD'S CHILDREN

3 1 Think of the love that the Father has lavished on us,
by letting us be called God's children;
and that is what we are.
Because the world refused to acknowledge him, (C2)
therefore it does not acknowledge us. (C2)
2 My dear people, we are already the children of God
but what we are to be in the future has not yet been revealed;
all we know is, that when it is revealed
we shall be like him
because we shall see him as he really is.

First condition: break with sin

3 Surely everyone who entertains this hope (C1)
must purify himself, must try to be as pure (C2)
as Christ.

1 JOHN

4 Anyone who sins at all (C2)
    breaks the law,
    because to sin is to break the law. (C2)
5 Now you know that he appeared in order (C2)
    to abolish sin,
    and that in him there is no sin; (C2)
6 anyone who lives in God does not sin, (C2)
    and anyone who sins (C2)
    has never seen him or known him.
7 My children, do not let anyone lead you astray: (C2)
    to live a holy life (C3)
    is to be holy just as he is holy; (C3)
8 to lead a sinful life is to belong to the devil,
    since the devil was a sinner from the beginning. (C2)
    It was to undo all that the devil has done
    that the Son of God appeared.
9 No one who has been begotten by God sins; (C1)
    because God's seed remains inside him, (C4)
    he cannot sin when he has been begotten by God. (C2)

**Second condition: keep the commandments,
especially the law of love**

10 In this way we distinguish the children of God
    from the children of the devil:
    anybody not living a holy life (C2)
    and not loving his brother (C2)
    is no child of God's.
11 This is the message
    as you heard it from the beginning:
    that we are to love one another; (C3)
12 not to be like Cain, who belonged to the Evil One (C2)
    and cut his brother's throat; (C2)
    cut his brother's throat simply for this reason,

1 JOHN

    that his own life was evil and his brother (c3)
      lived a good life.
13 You must not be surprised, brothers, (c2)
    when the world hates you;
14 we have passed out of death and into life,
    and of this we can be sure
    because we love our brothers. (c3)
15 If you refuse to love, you must remain (c2)
      dead;
    to hate your brother is to be a murderer, (c2)
    and murderers, as you know, do not have
      eternal life in them.
16 This has taught us love— (c3)
    that he gave up his life for us;
    and we, too, ought to give up our lives for (c3)
      our brothers.
17 If a man who was rich enough in this
      world's goods
    saw that one of his brothers was in need, (c2)
    but closed his heart to him,
    how could the love of God be living in
      him?
18 My children,
    our love is not to be just words or mere (c3)
      talk,
    but something real and active;
19 only by this can we be certain
    that we are children of the truth
    and be able to quieten our conscience in
      his presence,
20 whatever accusations it may raise against
      us,
    because God is greater than our con-
      science and he knows everything.
21 My dear people,
    if we cannot be condemned by our own
      conscience,
    we need not be afraid in God's presence,
22 and whatever we ask him,
    we shall receive,
    because we keep his commandments (c3)

and live the kind of life that he wants.
23 His commandments are these:
that we believe in the name of his Son Jesus Christ (c1)
and that we love one another (c3)
as he told us to.
24 Whoever keeps his commandments (c3)
lives in God and God lives in him.
We know that he lives in us
by the Spirit that he has given us.

Third condition: be on guard against the enemies of Christ and against the world

4 1 It is not every spirit, my dear people, that (c1)
you can trust;
test them, to see if they come from God;
there are many false prophets, now, in the world. (c2)
2 You can tell the spirits that come from God by this:
every spirit which acknowledges that Jesus the Christ has come in the flesh (c1)
is from God;
3 but any spirit which will not say this of Jesus
is not from God, (c2)
but is the spirit of Antichrist,
whose coming you were warned about. (c2)
Well, now he is here, in the world.
4 Children,

you have already overcome these false prophets,
because you are from God and you have in you (c2)
one who is greater than anyone in this world;
5 as for them, they are of the world, (c2)
and so they speak the language of the world
and the world listens to them.
6 But we are children of God,
and those who know God listen to us; (c1)
those who are not of God refuse to listen to us. (c3)
This is how we can tell (c2)
the spirit of truth from the spirit of falsehood.

III. LOVE AND FAITH

Love

7 My dear people,
let us love one another (c3)
since love comes from God (c3)
and everyone who loves is begotten by God and knows God.
8 Anyone who fails to love can never have known God, (c2)
because God is love.

Week 3 Day 4
Four C's Meditations
on 1 John 3:1-4:8

1. Most Sacred Heart of Jesus, the souls in Heaven, as St. John says in today's reading, see God as He is.(133) And St. Paul wrote, "Now we are seeing a dim reflection in a mirror; but then we shall be seeing face to face."(134) In this life we know God principally through faith, i.e., intellectual assent (belief) to what has been revealed to us about Him. In Heaven, however, we shall see Him directly, immediately, and intuitively as He is.

2. Yet, St. John cautions us that seeing God as He is requires purity, the type of purity You possess, Lord.

3. "Surely everyone who entertains this hope must purify himself, must try to be as pure as Christ."(135) In other words, we must constantly strive to be free of all deliberately willed sins.

4. How can we accomplish this? By applying the "Four C's Peaceful Seed-Living Formula" to our lives. A Christian exercising confidence (faith and hope) and seed-charity on a constant basis promotes and supports purity of conscience. And a pure conscience in turn promotes and supports confidence and seed-charity in this life, and a life of seed-charity in Heaven, accompanied by the intuitive, direct knowledge of God.

5. If we lead a life of constant faith and hope in God coupled with sacrificial love for God and neighbor, we will be crowding sin out of our consciences. And if we maintain pure consciences, through prayer and penance, for example, we will be making our souls more receptive to the supernatural virtues of faith, hope and seed-love.

6. Jesus, always give us the gift of purity, whereby we will be able to see You, the Father and the Holy Spirit face to face in Your heavenly Kingdom. *(See the "Beatific Vision," in "The Catholic Catechism," pp. 260-263.)*

7. Lord, St. John stresses repeatedly that Your true followers must be pure, that is, they must be holy if they are to see God. And You Yourself said, "Happy the pure in heart: they shall see God," and "You must be...perfect just as your heavenly Father is perfect."*(136, 137, 138)* While, we should not expect to be completely holy and perfect in this life, we should strive for that goal as long as we are here.

8. It will be good to remind ourselves at this point, Jesus, that to be holy is to dedicate one's self entirely to God through the power of Your grace. Thus, all our thoughts, words and actions are to be inspired and directed by You. To be holy then is not, as some believe, simply to be a "good" person. No, a holy person has a supernatural, transcendent, heavenly orientation to his life. His life is theocentric, i.e., God-centered. It is also Christo-centric or Christ-centered. We could

also say that it is spiritually centered on the Holy Spirit Who illuminates and inspires Your followers, Lord, and gives them Your graces.

9. Jesus, St. John wrote that some taught that You did not come in the flesh to bring us salvation.*(139)* In our own day, as we have already noted elsewhere, a false teaching regarding Your being and nature tends towards the opposite direction. That is, it holds, that You are only a man. Nonetheless, the equally false assertion that You are only a spiritual being reflects an attitude towards the material world that is also incorrectly maintained by some today.

10 Thus, there are some who find it inconceivable that God, a pure spirit, could have any direct contact with matter and material things. The implication is that material things are in some sense evil. This, of course, cannot be the case since You, Who are God the Son, and therefore entirely good, made everything in the universe, visible and invisible, material and spiritual. Clearly, some

material things are used for evil purposes, but matter itself is not evil.

11. As far as salvation is concerned, if You did not assume a complete human nature with a material body, as well as a spiritual soul, You did not redeem human nature. Therefore, You would not be the Savior of humanity.

12. Thankfully, Lord, You did take on human flesh and You did redeem our bodies and souls. You have also given us the grace to conquer the sin-oriented passions that reside in our flesh. May we always use this grace.

13. Jesus, St. John urged those for whom he wrote to "...love one another since love comes from God and everyone who loves is begotten by God and knows God. Anyone who fails to love can never have known God, because God is love."*(140)*

14. It is important for people to realize, Lord, that the love which St. John wrote about is not romantic love, nor is it simply a feeling of affection for others. Rather it is seed-charity or sacrificial love. It is a selfless

love, a love that seeks nothing simply for itself. And, as St. John said, God Himself is essentially this type of love. Moreover, it is from God that we receive the gift of seed-charity whereby we can give ourselves completely and selflessly to God and to our fellow human beings.

15. For many, it may seem an unattainable ideal that we should sacrifice ourselves completely to the divine will and for the good of others. But, thankfully, we have the example of thousands of saints, who in the past and in the present have, in fact, lived heroic lives of seed-charity.

16. Saints started out with the same human frailty we have, but through the constant and heroic use of seed-charity, each triumphed over evil. And we can also, Jesus, by making use of the seed-charity, won for us on the Cross, and obtainable through prayer and the sacraments You gave to Your Church.

17. Jesus, since seed-charity comes directly from God, it is not a part of our nature. It is a divine gift, and its presence within us no longer indicates that we are living only on the level of nature, but on a supernatural level in which we share in God's very own nature. Thus, Lord, as St. John also wrote, when we love with seed-charity, it is a sign that we have been begotten by God.*(141)* We have become His adopted children and are no longer simply His creatures.

18. Most Sacred Heart of Jesus, can we ever fully appreciate and understand this?

Those who live lives of sacrificial love are God's adopted children! God the Father becomes our Father and You become our Brother! And it is You Who have made this possible as the fruit of Your life of complete seed-charity while on earth. Thank You, Lord, and may our love for You never cease. Amen.

Please read and meditate on Chapter VIII, James 2:1-26 of Peaceful Seed Living, Volume I.

WEEK 3 DAY 5
The First Letter of St. John
Chapter 4:9-12

9   God's love for us was revealed
when God sent into the world his only Son
so that we could have life through him;
10 this is the love I mean:
not our love for God,   (C3)
but God's love for us when he sent his Son
to be the sacrifice that takes our sins away.

1 JOHN

11 My dear people,
   since God has loved us so much,
   we too should love one another. (C3)
12 No one has ever seen God;
   but as long as we love one another (C3)
   God will live in us
   and his love will be complete in us. (C3)

Week 3 Day 5
Four C's Meditations
on I John 4:9-12

1. Most Merciful Savior, St. John describes God (the Father) as being love (seed-charity), but he does not stop with a mere statement of the Father's principal attribute.*(142)* He also points out that it was in His act of sending You, His only-begotten Son, to earth to die for our sins that His love for mankind was revealed. And You, Lord, demonstrated Your love for the Father, and for us, by freely accepting the Father's will and by offering Yourself to the Father on the Cross.

2. "...I have come from heaven, not to do my own will, but to do the will of the one who sent me."*(143)*

3. "My Father...if it is possible, let this cup (of suffering) pass me by. Nevertheless, let it be as you, not I, would have it."*(144)*

4. We are called to imitate Your love for us, Jesus. And certainly this is possible with the aid of Your gift of seed-charity. But the fact is most of us Christians do not do so on a constant basis. There are times, lots of times, that we put the selfish love of ourselves in the place of the unselfish love for God and man. Yet how foolish this is, because when we do so we are flirting with death, spiritual death. May Your Holy Spirit point out to us, as often as is necessary, our folly in this regard. And may He inspire us to repent and amend our lives.

5. Jesus, St. John notes that "since God has loved us so much, we too should love one another. No one has ever seen God; but as long as we love one another God will live in us."*(145)*

6. That is to say, how much we really love God is measured by our acts of self-sacrifice for one another.

7. "When the Son of Man comes in his glory, escorted by all the angels then he will take his seat on this throne of glory. All the nations will be assembled before him and he will separate men from one another as the shepherds separate sheep from goats. He will place the sheep on his right hand and the goats on his left. Then the King will say to those on his right hand, 'Come, you whom my Father has blessed, take for your heritage the kingdom prepared for you since the foundation of the world. For I was hungry and you gave me food; I was thirsty and you gave

me drink; I was a stranger and you made me welcome; naked and you clothed me, sick and you visited me, in prison and you came to see me.' Then the virtuous will say to him in reply, 'Lord, when did we see you hungry and feed you; or thirsty and give you drink? When did we see you a stranger and make you welcome; naked and clothed you; sick and in prison and go to see you? And the King will answer, 'I tell you solemnly, in so far as you did this to one of the least of these brothers of mine, you did it to me.'"*(146)*

8. Genuine love of God, Jesus, is not simply a verbal commitment to the Persons of the Holy Trinity and to the divine will. It shows itself in concrete acts of self-sacrifice for our fellow man. And if our motives for helping them are pure, that is, if we do it primarily out of love for God, and for our fellow man for God's sake, then God will be living in us. The Father, the Son and the Holy Spirit will be making their dwelling place in us, and They will be promoting our sanctity still further by continuously inspiring us to help others in need.

9. Lord Jesus, frequently the neediest people we encounter are those closest to us; members of our immediate families, relatives, friends, co-workers, etc. Yet, we may sometimes be blind to their needs through our neglect, that is, through neglecting to take the time to assess their real needs and then asking ourselves in what ways can we help meet them.

10. Have we considered, for example, whether there are any close to us who are very lonely? If there are, have we contributed to their loneliness? Have we spent enough time with our spouses, children, or parents? Do we speak to them often and in a gentle manner?

11. What about the problem of spiritual impoverishment? Have we contributed sufficiently to the spiritual needs of others? Have we prayed daily for and with our families? Have we contributed regularly to the spiritual and moral education of our children? Most of us wish to do all in our power to keep our families from being materially poor, but what about their spiritual needs?

12. Are there widows, widowers, handicapped, or jobless people in our neighborhood? Have we visited them or prayed for them?

13. We could go on and on like this, Lord, but we need not do so here. Nonetheless it is good from time to time to assess the needs of those closest to us, and if possible, to help them in the attainment of their needs. "Insofar as you did this to one of the least of these brothers of mine, you did it to me."*(147)*

14. Most Sacred Heart of Jesus, help us always to be alert to the needs of others and inspire us to help them according to Your will. Amen.

Try to read these Scripture passages and meditations several times a day in a reflective manner. Each time you do so, the Holy Spirit will give you more insights.

Please read and meditate on Chapter VIII, James 3:1-12 of Peaceful Seed Living, Volume I.

WEEK 3 DAY 6
The First Letter of St. John
Chapters 4:13-5:21

13 We can know that we are living in him
and he is living in us
because he lets us share his Spirit.
14 We ourselves saw and we testify
that the Father sent his Son (C1)
as savior of the world.
15 If anyone acknowledges that Jesus is the Son of God,
God lives in him, and he in God. (C1)
16 We ourselves have known and put our faith in
God's love toward ourselves. (C1)
God is love
and anyone who lives in love lives in God, (C3)
and God lives in him.
17 Love will come to its perfection in us (C3)
when we can face the day of Judgment without fear;
because even in this world
we have become as he is.

1 JOHN

18 In love there can be no fear,
 but fear is driven out by perfect love: (C3)
 because to fear is to expect punishment, (C3)
 and anyone who is afraid is still imperfect (C3)
 in love.
19 We are to love, then,
 because he loved us first. (C3)
20 Anyone who says, "I love God," (C2)
 and hates his brother,
 is a liar,
 since a man who does not love the brother (C2)
 that he can see
 cannot love God, whom he has never (C3)
 seen.
21 So this is the commandment that he has
 given us,
 that anyone who loves God must also love
 his brother.

1 Whoever believes that Jesus is the Christ (C1)
5 has been begotten by God;
 and whoever loves the Father that begot (C3)
 him
 loves the child whom he begets.
2 We can be sure that we love God's chil- (C3)
 dren
 if we love God himself and do what he has (C3)
 commanded us; (C3)
3 this is what loving God is—
 keeping his commandments;
4 and his commandments are not difficult,
 because anyone who has been begotten by
 God
 has already overcome the world;
 this is the victory over the world— (C1)
 our faith.

Faith

5 Who can overcome the world?
 Only the man who believes that Jesus is (C1)
 the Son of God:

1 JOHN

6 Jesus Christ who came by water and blood,[a]
not with water only,
but with water and blood;
with the Spirit as another witness—
since the Spirit is the truth—
7 so that there are three witnesses,
8 the Spirit, the water and the blood,
and all three of them agree.
9 We accept the testimony of human witnesses,
but God's testimony is much greater,
and this is God's testimony,
given as evidence for his Son.
10 Everybody who believes in the Son of God (C1)
has this testimony inside him;
and anyone who will not believe God (C2)
is making God out to be a liar,
because he has not trusted (C1)
the testimony God has given about his Son.
11 This is the testimony:
God has given us eternal life
and this life is in his Son;
12 anyone who has the Son has life, (C3)
anyone who does not have the Son does not have life.

Conclusion

13 I have written all this to you (C1)
so that you who believe in the name of the Son of God
may be sure that you have eternal life.

ENDING

---

5 a. The water and the blood from the side of Jesus, Jn 19:34, are here used as figures of his "coming" to all Christians, through the water of baptism and through his sacrificial death.

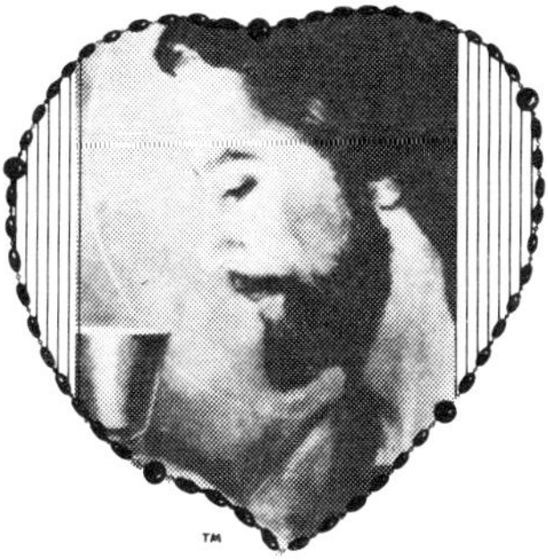

Prayer for sinners

14 We are quite confident that if we ask him for anything, (c1)
and it is in accordance with his will,
he will hear us;
15 and, knowing that whatever we may ask, he hears us, (c1)
we know that we have already been granted what we asked of him.
16 If anybody sees his brother commit a sin (c2)
that is not a deadly sin, (c2)
he has only to pray, and God will give life to the sinner
—not those who commit a deadly sin; (c2)
for there is a sin that is death,
and I will not say that you must pray about that. (c2)
17 Every kind of wrong-doing is sin,
but not all sin is deadly. (c2)

Summary of the letter

18 We know that anyone who has been begotten by God
does not sin, (c2)
because the begotten Son of God protects him,
and the Evil One does not touch him. (c2)
19 We know that we belong to God,
but the whole world lies in the power of the Evil One.

1 JOHN

20 We know, too, that the Son of God has come,
and has given us the power
to know the true God. (C1)
We are in the true God,
as we are in his Son, Jesus Christ. (C3)
This is the true God,
this is eternal life.
21 Children, be on your guard against false gods.

**Week 3 Day 6
Four C's Meditations
on 1 John 4:13-5:21**

1. In today's Scripture reading, Jesus, St. John speaks of the incompatibility of sacrificial love and fear.

2. "Love will come into perfection in us

when we can face the day of Judgment without fear; because even in this world we have become as he is. In love there can be no fear, but fear is driven out by perfect love: because to fear is to expect punishment, and anyone who is afraid is still imperfect in love."*(148)*

3. Quite simply then, if we possessed perfect love we would rise above serving God just to avoid His punishment. Our sole motive for turning to God would be our love for Him. *(For a disussion on an aspect of this perfect love, see "The Catholic Catechism," pp.489-490.)*

4. Lord, our sins, especially our unrepented sins, are the very basis for our legitimate fear of divine punishment. Therefore, grant that we may love You with a love so perfect that deliberate sins become unthinkable.

5. Jesus, in chapter five St. John speaks once more of the importance of faith for salvation, wherein we are "begotten by God."*(149)* But the impression should not be given that He is saying that faith alone is sufficient. We have already seen in chapter four that St. John insists that love (seed-charity) is necessary as well.

6. "My dear people, let us love one another since love comes from God and everyone who loves is begotten by God and knows God."*(150)*

7. We could say then that faith is an essential vehicle for salvation, but supernatural charity is needed to perfect or

consecrate the process of salvation.

8. St. John tells us in his Gospel that Baptism is also required for salvation, since You have given us this sacrament, Lord, as the means whereby we receive both faith and charity, along with many other gifts and privileges.

9. "I tell you most solemnly, unless a man is born from above, he cannot see the kingdom of God.... I tell you most solemnly, unless a man is born through water and the Spirit (Baptism) he cannot enter the kingdom of God."*(151)*

10. And St. Peter said that in order to be saved "you must repent...everyone of you must be baptized in the name of Jesus Christ for the forgiveness of your sins, and you will receive the gift of the Holy Spirit.*(152)*

11. Lord, may we never lack in Your gifts of faith and seed-charity through which we are given entrance into Your Kingdom of Heaven and the enjoyment of Your friendship even while living on earth.

12. Jesus, St. John also tells us that we cannot overcome the world of evil that constantly confronts us except through belief in You as the Son of God.*(153)* Here we see once more the insistence that You are not only a man but also God, the Second Person of the Holy Trinity. If You were only man, even a sinless man, You would not be able to save others from their sins. Only God can do that. And if You were only a sinless man, that in itself would not gain even Yourself

entrance into Heaven and God's friendship.

13. Heaven and divine friendship are gifts from God alone. No creature, no matter how perfect, can have a natural claim on them. Man has no more right, as man, to Heaven than has a snail. Furthermore, our sinful condition has compounded the difficulty of living in God's presence and in His love forever.

14. Thankfully, Lord, You are the Son of God. You are the perfect man. You are the Messiah Who sacrificed Yourself on the altar of the Cross for our salvation. May we show our true thankfulness by applying Scripture's *"Four C's Formula for Peaceful Seed Living"* to our own lives. And by doing so we will attract others to You and to their salvation.

15. Jesus, St. John clarifies a problem some have about prayer. They say that they have prayed for one thing or another and their prayers were not answered. Actually, in such instances, You may well have responded in a positive manner, but not as soon as or in the way those praying might have liked. On the

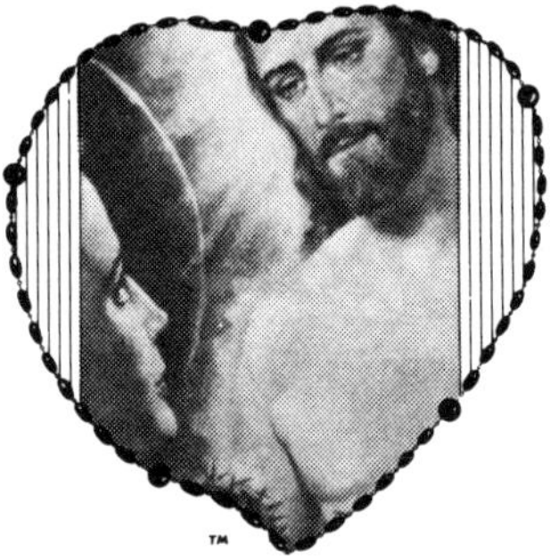

other hand, what was prayed for might not have been according to Your Will, and was therefore refused. The refusal may have been due to personal sinfulness, or for a multitude of other reasons. Anyway, St. John makes his point clear: for prayers to be answered as we would like them to be answered, the request must be according to Your Will.

16. "We are quite confident that if we ask Him (the Son of God) for anything, and it is in accordance to his will, he will hear us; and, knowing that whatever we may ask, he hears us, we know that we have already been granted what we asked of him.*(154)*

17. Jesus, with the assistance of Your Holy Spirit, please help us to pray only for those things that are pleasing to You, and grant us patience while waiting for Your response. May we make our own the words You prayed in the Garden of Gethsemene. "My Father.... Let it be as You, not I, would have it."*(155)*

18. Lord, St. John makes a distinction in chapter five between a sin that is deadly (mortal) and one which is not deadly

(venial).*(156)* A deadly sin is one which robs the individual of the supernatural life and of Your favor and friendship. Also when a mortal sin is present sanctifying grace and seed-charity, which are vital for the supernatural life, are removed. And, unfortunately, the prayers of others cannot obtain forgiveness for those who commit mortal sins. On the other hand, their prayers might be the means by which an individual is lead to repentance and to the confession of the mortal sin, and therefore becomes restored to the supernatural state. *(For further information on mortal and venial sins, see "The Catholic Catechism," pp. 180-184.)*

19. Finally, Lord, St. John makes the statement that those who have been begotten by God do not sin because they are protected by You.*(157)* It would seem significant that St. John did not say that those begotten by God could not sin. He only said that they do not sin. In other words, it appears that St. John means that (mortal) sin, or grave sin deliberately committed, is not characteristic of the adopted children of God, for if anyone committed a mortal sin, he would no longer be one of God's begotten ones.

20. Lord, help us to realize that those in a saving relationship with God do not commit mortal sins. Yet, if they were to do so, they would no longer be in the state of grace. Enable us to realize, too, that venial sins do not destroy our saving relationship with You, although they certainly weaken it. But, more

importantly, if we take no steps to check them, especially fully deliberate venial sins, they can lead us to commit mortal sins. The principal point we wish to stress here, however, is that it would appear that St. John did not have reference to venial sins when he wrote that those begotten of God do not sin.

21. Lord, You Who protect the begotten ones of God from sinning, please inspire us to seek Your protection daily, so that we may remain in the Father's friendship forever. Amen.

Try to read these Scripture passages and meditation several times a day in a reflective manner. Each time you do so, the Holy Spirit will give you more insights.

Please read and meditate on Chapter VIII, James 3:13- 5:20 of Peaceful Seed Living, Volume I.

WEEK 3 DAY 7
The Second & Third Letters of St. John
2 John 1-13   3 John 1-15

2 John

THE SECOND LETTER OF JOHN

1 From the Elder: my greetings to the Lady, the chosen one,[a] and to her children, she whom I love in the truth—and I am not the only one, for so do all who have come to
2 know the truth—·because of the truth that lives in us and will be with us for ever.
3 In our life of truth and love, we shall have grace, mercy and peace from God the Father and from Jesus Christ, the Son of the Father.

The law of love

4 It has given me great joy to find that your children have been living the life of truth as
5 we were commanded by the Father. ·I am writing now, dear lady, not to give you any new commandment, but the one which **we** were given at the beginning, and to plead: **let** us love one another.
6 To love is to live according to his commandments: this is the commandment which you have heard since the beginning, to live a life of love.

---

1 a. The local church to which the letter is addressed.

2 JOHN

The enemies of Christ

7 There are many deceivers about in the world, refusing to admit that Jesus Christ has come in the flesh. They are the Deceiver; 8 they are the Antichrist. ·Watch yourselves, or all our work will be lost and not get the 9 reward it deserves. ·If anybody does not keep within the teaching of Christ but goes beyond it, he cannot have God with him: only those who keep to what he taught can have the 10 Father and the Son with them. ·If anyone comes to you bringing a different doctrine, you must not receive him in your house or 11 even give him a greeting. ·To greet him would make you a partner in his wicked work.

12 There are several things I have to tell you, but I have thought it best not to trust them **to paper** and ink. I hope instead to visit you **and talk** to you personally, so that our joy **may be** complete.

13 **Greetings** to you from the children of your sister,[b] the chosen one.

3 John

THE THIRD LETTER OF JOHN

1 From the Elder: greetings to my dear friend 2 Gaius, whom I love in the truth. ·My dear friend, I hope everything is going happily with you and that you are as well physically

---

b. The local church from which the letter is sent.

3 as you are spiritually. ·It was a great joy to me when some brothers came and told of your faithfulness to the truth, and of your life **4** in the truth. ·It is always my greatest joy to hear that my children are living according to the truth.

5 My friend, you have done faithful work in looking after these brothers, even though **6** they were complete strangers to you. ·They are a proof to the whole Church of your charity and it would be a very good thing if you could help them on their journey in a way **7** that God would approve. ·It was entirely for the sake of the name that they set out, without **8** depending on the pagans for anything; ·it is our duty to welcome men of this sort and contribute our share to their work for the truth.

Beware of the example of Diotrephes

9 I have written a note for the members of the church, but Diotrephes, who seems to enjoy being in charge of it, refuses to accept **10** us. ·So if I come, I shall tell everyone how he has behaved, and about the wicked accusations he has been circulating against us. As if that were not enough, he not only refuses to welcome our brothers, but prevents the other people who would have liked to from doing it, and expels them from the church.

3 JOHN

11 My dear friend, never follow such a bad example, but keep following the good one; anyone who does what is right is a child of God, but the person who does what is wrong has never seen God. (c2) (c4) (c3) (c2)

Commendation of Demetrius

12 Demetrius has been approved by everyone, and indeed by the truth itself. We too will vouch for him and you know that our testimony is true.

Epilogue

13 There are several things I had to tell you but I would rather not trust them to pen and (c3)
14 ink. ·However, I hope to see you soon and
15 talk to you personally. ·Peace be with you; greetings from your friends; greet each of our (c3) friends by name.

Week 3 Day 7
Four C's Meditations
on 2 John 1-13   3 John 1-15

1. Lord, if St. Paul can be referred to as the Apostle of faith, because of his emphasis on this supernatural virtue in his writings, St. John can certainly be called the Apostle of love (seed-charity) due to his stress on this particular gift of God. Examples of this are clearly seen in today's Scripture readings.

2. St. John begins both his Second and Third Letters with references to Christians "whom I love in the truth."*(158)* Here, "love" undoubtedly means the sacrificial seed-charity which comes from You, Lord, Who are the Truth. It is through our union with You in Baptism that we are able to love others sacrificially. Thus perfect love is that which loves without seeking or expecting something in return. And it is this love that is capable of loving unselfishly, without counting the cost, even to the point of death. Those who love in this manner are loving in the Truth.*(159)*

3. This sacrificial love, as should be apparent, Jesus, is more than romantic love which is based on instinct and is ultimately intended for marriage and the begetting of children. Nor is this sacrificial seed-charity merely the love of human friendship, as such, since this latter type of love depends on mutual justice and respect. Thus, if injustice, or the lack of respect for one or the other

friends enters the picture, the love of friendship ceases.

4. A person having seed-charity, on the other hand, loves all people including those he dislikes and even regards as his enemies. Persons having seed-charity are able to love everyone with the intent of doing all they can to either bring them to Your salvation, or to maintain them in that saving relationship.

5. Lord, inspire us always to use the gift of seed-charity to the greatest degree possible, in any situation, since this is a gift that cannot be used too frequently or over-indulged in. May we see all our fellow human beings as potential saints, and do all that we reasonably can to help them obtain this goal.

6. Jesus, St. John also assures us that, "In our life of truth and love, we shall have grace, mercy and peace from God the Father, and from Jesus Christ, the Son of the Father.*(160)* Here we see at least a partial allusion to the *"Four C's Formula for Peaceful Seed Living."*

7. In the first instance, we must have confidence (faith), Lord, if we are to maintain ourselves in the Truth, whether the Truth refers to You personally or to Your saving doctrine of salvation. The love mentioned above, is of course, seed-charity. And if we have the grace of seed-charity within us, our consciences are free from at least mortal sins, since seed-charity and mortal sin cannot coexist in a person. Therefore, a Christian life based on the Truth and seed-charity

necessarily implies a pure conscience, i.e., a conscience free of the stains of mortal sin. And if this Christian life is to be maintained it needs the gift of constancy. Lastly, we note that St. John states that those who live in Truth and in love will obtain God's peace, along with His mercy and grace. And it is this peace of God that The Apostolate for Family Consecration promotes and urges its members to receive through practicing the Four C's Formula.

8. Jesus, we also found in today's meditation another indirect reference to constancy. St. John warned against false teachers who deceive true believers into accepting doctrine which did not come from You. Then he wrote:

9. "Watch yourselves, or all our work will be lost and not get the reward it deserves. If anybody does not keep within the teaching of Christ but goes beyond it, he cannot have God with him: only those who keep to what he taught can have the Father and the Son with them."*(161)*

10. Here then constancy in faith is clearly called for, otherwise those who have once fully accepted what You taught, with the gift of faith, will be in danger of accepting false doctrine, and therefore of losing faith which is essential for salvation.

11. Most Sacred Heart of Jesus, if we are to persevere in faith, and also in seed-charity, we must have constancy. Help us not to lose it so that our friendship with You will continue to the end when we will be confirmed in your reward of eternal life.

12. Lord, in his Third Letter, St. John praised those for whom he wrote because they had sacrificed themselves for some previously unknown missionaries. John concluded by saying "...it is our duty to welcome men of this sort and contribute our share to their work for the truth."*(162)* This reminds us of St. Paul's statement that we should do good to everyone, but especially to one's brothers in the faith.

13. "We must never get tired of doing good because if we don't give up the struggle we shall get our harvest at the proper time. While we have the chance, we must do good to all, and especially to our brothers in the faith."(163)

14. Certainly, Lord, we are to be charitable to all, but we must be especially mindful of members of our families and our fellow believers who are linked to us in Your Mystical Body, the Church. For many of us, however, it is easier to be charitable to those whom we know only at a distance than towards those with whom we come in constant contact. It seems that it is these latter persons who irritate us far more often and who sometimes even make unreasonable, if not impossible, demands of us.

15. Perhaps the acid test of Christian living is to be found in the setting of our homes. How easy it is, Lord, to let "our hair down" at home and take family members for granted. How easy it is to shirk all pretense of politeness for one another, and to say what we are thinking without any regard for the feelings of others, and to complain, and quarrel, and to get on one another's nerves through our lack of consideration, and to yell and even scream at one another. Yet as Sir Thomas Browne put it, "Charity begins at home...."* Yes, if we cannot be charitable at home, isn't it likely that what passes as charity towards others outside the home is only a veneer, inspired more by "enlightened

self-interest," than by God the Holy Spirit? (*Religio medici*, Part 2, Section 4.)

16. Jesus, we humbly ask You to help us be charitable, day in and day out, with all the members of our family and community. Also help us realize that those who are most unlovable are precisely those in most need of our seeds of self-sacrifice. And may we never cease to pray fervently for each family member, seeking Your continual blessing upon them. Amen.

Try to read these Scripture passages and meditations several times a day in a reflective manner. Each time you do so, the Holy Spirit will give you more insights.

Please read Chapter IX, Paragraphs 1 to 11 (end) of Peaceful Seed Living, Volume I.

References to Scripture

(1)   John 1:1
(2)   John 1:1
(3)   John 1:9
(4)   John 1:7
(5)   Matthew 10:33
(6)   Matthew 25:14-30
(7)   John 1:27-29
(8)   1 Peter 3:18
(9)   Roman 5:6-8
(10) John 15:13
(11) John 2:11
(12) John 2:23
(13) Mark 16:20
(14) John 2:13-22
(15) 1 Corinthians 6:13-20
(16) Matthew 15:18-20
(17) 2 Timothy 2:21
(18) John 3:1-15
(19) Matthew 28:20
(20) John 3:30-31
(21) Galatians 2:20
(22) John 4:5-42
(23) Galatians 5:19-21
(24) 1 Corinthians 9:6-20
(25) John 4:23-24
(26) Matthew 28:20 John 14:23
(27) Luke 16:18; Romans 7:1-3
(28) John 5:14
(29) John 9:3
(30) John 5:24

(31) Acts 2:38
(32) John 3:5
(33) James 2:14,17,26
(34) Galatians 5:5-6
(35) 1 John 5:16-17
(36) 1 Corinthians 13:1-3
(37) John 6:48-58
(38) John 6:64-68
(39) John 7:37-38
(40) John 7:38-39
(41) John 4:14
(42) Matthew 23:23-24
(43) John 8:23
(44) John 15:18-19
(45) John 12:31;14:30;16:11
(46) John 8:31-32
(47) John 8:43-45
(48) John 14:6
(49) 1 Peter 5:8-9
(50) John 9:24-25,28-34
(51) John 10:1-21
(52) Acts 4:14
(53) John 10:27-30
(55) John 10:34
(56) John 11:1-44
(57) John 11:25
(58) 1 Corinthians 15:12;20-29
(59) John 12:11,14-15,42,45
(60) John 11:5,32-36
(61) John 11:33
(62) Matthew 26:6
(63) Luke 18:18-23
(64) Luke 4:18
(65) John 12:23-32
(66) 2 Peter 1:4
(67) Matthew 16:24

(68) John 12:36
(69) Matthew 16:18-19; 18:18
(70) John 12:35
(71) Matthew 8:12
(72) John 12:42-43
(73) Matthew 25:30
(74) Luke 9:26
(75) John 13:1-6
(76) John 13:17
(77) John 13:21-30
(78) Matthew 25:41-46
(79) John 13:34
(80) Romans 5:7-9
(81) John 14:1
(82) Matthew 6:27-34
(83) John 14:6
(84) John 14:12
(85) John 14:15-17
(86) John 14:13
(87) John 14:15
(88) John 14:21-23
(89) 1 Corinthians 6:19
(90) John 14:27
(91) John 15:1-8
(92) John 15:18-20
(93) James 4:4
(94) Matthew 10:23
(95) 1 Corinthians 10:13
(96) 2 Corinthians 12:9
(97) John 16:33
(98) John 17:18-21
(99) Romans 5:8
(100) Luke 6:31-35
(101) Matthew 7:3-5
(102) John 13:38
(103) Acts 2

(104) John 19:1-6
(105) John 15:13
(106) Romans 5:8
(107) Luke 23:34
(108) Galatians 6:10
(109) Matthew 28:11-15
(110) Acts 5:27-33; 1 Corinthians 15; 1 Corinthians 11:16-33
(111) John 20:20-21
(112) Acts 9:16
(113) John 14:27, Matthew 16:24
(114) Acts 5:40-41
(115) John 20:21
(116) John 20:22-23
(117) John 20:24-29
(118) John 20:28
(119) John 21:15-19
(120) Luke 22:21-34
(121) Matthew 16:18
(122) Matthew 16:16-19
(123) Matthew 28:16-20
(124) 1 John 1:3-4
(125) 1 John 1:8-10
(126) Hebrews 4:15
(127) Romans 5:12
(128) 1 John 2:5-6
(129) 1 John 2:9-10
(130) 1 John 2:15
(131) 1 John 2:16
(132) John 3:30
(133) 1 John 3:2
(134) 1 Corinthians 13:12
(135) 1 John 3:3
(136) 1 John 3:7

(137) Matthew 5:8
(138) Matthew 5:48
(139) 1 John 4:2-3
(140) 1 John 4:7-8
(141) 1 Peter 1:4
(142) 1 John 4:8,16
(143) John 6:38
(144) Matthew 26:29-40
(145) 1 John 4:11-12
(146) Matthew 25:31-40
(147) Matthew 25:31-40
(148) 1 John 4:17-18
(149) 1 John 5:1
(150) 1 John 4:7
(151) John 3:3-5
(152) Acts 2:38
(153) 1 John 5:5
(154) 1 John 5:14-15
(155) Matthew 26:39
(156) 1 John 5:16-17
(157) 1 John 5:18
(158) 2 John 1; 3 John 1
(159) John 14:6
(160) 2 John 3
(161) 2 John 8-9
(162) 3 John 8
(163) Galatians 6:9-10

OFFICERS AND STAFF

Jerome F. Coniker
President — Founder
Gwen C. Coniker
Wife, Mother and Author
Rev. William J. Dorney
Vice President
Dale Francis
Journalist — Program Editor
John W. Hand
Vice President — Co-Founder
Rev. John A. Hardon, S.J.
Theological Advisor
Mother Immaculata, H.M.C.
AFC Program Author
William J. Isaacson
Vice President and Asst. Secretary
Rev. Lawrence G. Lovasik, S.V.D.
AFC Program Author
Francis J. Milligan, Jr.
Vice President & Treasurer
Rev. Thomas A. Morrison, O.P.
Thomistic Advisor
Dr. Thomas A. Prier, M.D.
Secretary — Co-Founder
Dr. Burns K. Seeley, Ph.D.
Vice President — Staff Theologian
Sr. John Vianney, S.S.N.D.
First Suffering Sacri-State Member Author and Program Advisor

ADVISORY COUNCIL

John Joseph Cardinal Carberry, D.D.
Former Archbishop of Saint Louis
Mario Luigi Cardinal Ciappi, O.P.
Official Theologian of the Supreme Pontiff
Archbishop Augustine P. Mayer, O.S.B.
Secretary, The Sacred Congregation for Religious & Secular Institutes
Bishop Leo J. Brust, D.D.
Vicar General Archdiocese of Milwaukee
Rev. Gabriel Calvo
Founder of Marriage Encounter
Sister Concetta, D.S.P.
Supreme Daughters of St. Paul
Raymond E. Cross
President Federal Chicago Corp.
Mother David Marie, H.P.B.
Mother General
Dr. Richard A. DeGraff, Ed.D.
Administrator and Educator
John F. Fink
President Our Sunday Visitor
Frank Flick
President Flick Reedy Corp.
Rev. Robert J. Fox
Pastor, Author, Journalist
Rev. Bernard M. Geiger, O.F.M. Conv.
Nat'l. Dir. Knights of Immaculata
W. Doyle Gilligan
Publisher Lumen Christi Press
Mr. & Mrs. L. D. Hawbaker
Parents of 11 children
Rev. Francis J. Kamp, S.V.D.
Nat'l. Miss. Dir. Divine Word Missionaries
Rev. Francis Larkin, SS.CC.*
Founder of our Home Visitation Sacred Heart Program
Rev. Paul A. Lenz
Exc. Dir. Bur. of Catholic Indian Missions
August J. Mauge*
Former Treasurer and Co-Founder
Rev. Robert J. McAllister, S.J.
Nat'l. Dir. Apostleship of Prayer
Rev. Vincent McCann
Reg. Superior Mill Hill Fathers
Rev. William G. Most, Ph.D.
Theologian, Author, Journalist
Rev. James I. O'Connor, S.J.
Canon Lawyer
Very Rev. Gabriel Pausback, O. Carm.
Writer & Former Assistant General
Howard V. Phalin
Former Pres. World Book Encyclopedia
Rev. Howard Rafferty, O. Carm.
Nat'l. Dir. Scapular Center
John E. Schaeffer
Attorney
Charles F. Scholl
The Dr. Scholl Foundation
Mr. and Mrs. William A. Spencer
President Spencer Bowling Lanes Wife, Mother and Lecturer
Mother Teresa of Calcutta
Foundress of the Missionaries of Charity and our Suffering Sacri-State Member Program

*Deceased

This prayer and recommended practices book is dedicated to The Sacred and Merciful Heart of Jesus for the renewal of family life throughout the world.

Reply Section

1. ( ) Please place this petition at the foot of the altar in your Sacred Hearts Chapel and include it in all of the Masses said for the needs of your petitioners throughout the coming week. Also include these petitions in your vigil of prayer on Fridays, particulary on First Fridays when your president spends his day or night before Our Eucharistic Lord praying for the intentions of all petitions received throughout the month.

_____
_____
_____
_____
_____
_____
_____
_____
_____
_____

2.a ( ) I promise to pray that God will use The Apostolate to inspire people to become an instrument to renew the family and the entire world in Jesus Christ. I would like to be listed as a Sacri-State member and participate in the spiritual benefits of The Apostolate.

2b ( ) I am a priest, and will include the intentions of The Apostolate and all of those who are asking for your prayers in my available Masses, particularly on Fridays.

3. ( ) Enclosed is my best for God, my seed-Charity donation for the vital work of The Apostolate. _____

4. ( ) Enclosed is a list of names of people who should be interested in The Apostolate.

5. ( ) I am not on your mailing list, please add my name.

6. ( ) Please notify me when you start to organize chapters in my area.

7. ( ) I would like to receive more information about Cooperator membership.

8. ( ) Please send your order form for your prayer books and materials.

Please Print:

Name: _____

Address: _____

City & State: _____

Zip: _____

The Apostolate, Box 220, Kenosha, WI 53141

Reply Section

1.. ( ) Please place this petition at the foot of the altar in your Sacred Hearts Chapel and include it in all of the Masses said for the needs of your petitioners throughout the coming week. Also include these petitions in your vigil of prayer on Fridays, particulary on First Fridays when your president spends his day or night before Our Eucharistic Lord praying for the intentions of all petitions received throughout the month.

———————————————
———————————————
———————————————
———————————————
———————————————
———————————————
———————————————
———————————————
———————————————
———————————————

2.a ( ) I promise to pray that God will use The Apostolate to inspire people to become an instrument to renew the family and the entire world in Jesus Christ. I would like to be listed as a Sacri-State member and participate in the spiritual benefits of The Apostolate.

2b ( ) I am a priest, and will include the intentions of The Apostolate and all of those who are asking for your prayers in my available Masses, particularly on Fridays.

3. ( ) Enclosed is my best for God, my seed-Charity donation for the vital work of The Apostolate. _____

4. ( ) Enclosed is a list of names of people who should be interested in The Apostolate.

5. ( ) I am not on your mailing list, please add my name.

6. ( ) Please notify me when you start to organize chapters in my area.

7. ( ) I would like to receive more information about Cooperator membership.

8. ( ) Please send your order form for your prayer books and materials.

Please Print:

Name: _____

Address: _____

City & State: _____

Zip: _____

The Apostolate, Box 220, Kenosha, WI 53141

Reply Section

1. ( ) Please place this petition at the foot of the altar in your Sacred Hearts Chapel and include it in all of the Masses said for the needs of your petitioners throughout the coming week. Also include these petitions in your vigil of prayer on Fridays, particulary on First Fridays when your president spends his day or night before Our Eucharistic Lord praying for the intentions of all petitions received throughout the month.

_____

_____

_____

_____

_____

_____

_____

_____

_____

2.a ( ) I promise to pray that God will use The Apostolate to inspire people to become an instrument to renew the family and the entire world in Jesus Christ. I would like to be listed as a Sacri-State member and participate in the spiritual benefits of The Apostolate.

2b ( ) I am a priest, and will include the intentions of The Apostolate and all of those who are asking for your prayers in my available Masses, particularly on Fridays.

3. ( ) Enclosed is my best for God, my seed-Charity donation for the vital work of The Apostolate. _____

4. ( ) Enclosed is a list of names of people who should be interested in The Apostolate.

5. ( ) I am not on your mailing list, please add my name.

6. ( ) Please notify me when you start to organize chapters in my area.

7. ( ) I would like to receive more information about Cooperator membership.

8. ( ) Please send your order form for your prayer books and materials.

Please Print:

Name: _____

Address: _____

City & State: _____

Zip: _____

The Apostolate, Box 220, Kenosha, WI 53141